The Slave Wars

A Captivating Guide to the Servile Wars and Spartacus

© Copyright 2021

All Rights Reserved. No part of this book may be reproduced in any form without permission in writing from the author. Reviewers may quote brief passages in reviews.

Disclaimer: No part of this publication may be reproduced or transmitted in any form or by any means, mechanical or electronic, including photocopying or recording, or by any information storage and retrieval system, or transmitted by email without permission in writing from the publisher.

While all attempts have been made to verify the information provided in this publication, neither the author nor the publisher assumes any responsibility for errors, omissions or contrary interpretations of the subject matter herein.

This book is for entertainment purposes only. The views expressed are those of the author alone, and should not be taken as expert instruction or commands. The reader is responsible for his or her own actions.

Adherence to all applicable laws and regulations, including international, federal, state and local laws governing professional licensing, business practices, advertising and all other aspects of doing business in the US, Canada, UK or any other jurisdiction is the sole responsibility of the purchaser or reader.

Neither the author nor the publisher assumes any responsibility or liability whatsoever on the behalf of the purchaser or reader of these materials. Any perceived slight of any individual or organization is purely unintentional.

Free Bonus from Captivating History (Available for a Limited time)

Hi History Lovers!

Now you have a chance to join our exclusive history list so you can get your first history ebook for free as well as discounts and a potential to get more history books for free! Simply visit the link below to join.

Captivatinghistory.com/ebook

Also, make sure to follow us on Facebook, Twitter and Youtube by searching for Captivating History.

Contents

PART 1: THE SERVILE WARS 1
    INTRODUCTION 2
    CHAPTER 1 - SLAVERY IN ROME 7
    CHAPTER 2 - THE FOUNDATIONS OF REBELLION (OR A
    BRIEF HISTORY OF THE ISLAND OF SICILY) 13
    CHAPTER 3 - EUNUS AND HIS PROPHECY 18
    CHAPTER 4 - THE FIRST SERVILE WAR 22
    CHAPTER 5 - THE CIMBRIAN WAR: CATALYST FOR THE
    SECOND SERVILE WAR 32
    CHAPTER 6 - THE ROMANS NEED AN ARMY 37
    CHAPTER 7 - THE SECOND SERVILE WAR 46
    CHAPTER 8 - GLADIATORS AND THEIR LIVES 57
    CHAPTER 9 - THE GLADIATORS WHO WOULD SHAKE
    ROME 66
    CHAPTER 10 - THE THIRD SERVILE WAR 71
    CONCLUSION 87
PART 2: SPARTACUS 91
    INTRODUCTION 93
    CHAPTER 1 - THRACE AND ITS ENEMIES 95
    CHAPTER 2 - ON THE ROMANS' SIDE 102
    CHAPTER 3 - SOLD 107

- CHAPTER 4 – THE REAL GLADIATOR 114
- CHAPTER 5 – AMBUSH 120
- CHAPTER 6 – FACING THE LEGIONS.. 127
- CHAPTER 7 – THE LONE VOLUNTEER 135
- CHAPTER 8 – AT THE FEET OF THE ALPS...................................... 140
- CHAPTER 9 – DEFEAT 146
- CHAPTER 10 – BETRAYED BY THE PIRATES 153
- CHAPTER 11 – CRASSUS' WALL.. 160
- CHAPTER 12 – THE LAST STAND.. 167
- CHAPTER 13 – AFTERMATH.. 172
- CHAPTER 14 – LEGACY 178
- CONCLUSION... 183

HERE'S ANOTHER BOOK BY CAPTIVATING HISTORY THAT YOU MIGHT LIKE 186
FREE BONUS FROM CAPTIVATING HISTORY (AVAILABLE FOR A LIMITED TIME) 187
SOURCES.. 188

Part 1: The Servile Wars

A Captivating Guide to the Three Slave Revolts Against the Roman Republic

Introduction

Ancient republics were formed on the philosophies of politicians and great minds while also being built on the backs of human exploitation. For centuries, every great empire or kingdom was (and still is) divided between the powerful elite and the working class. But even with that division, there was still one class that sat below them all—slaves. Those poor individuals who found themselves at the bottom of the ladder were forced to do the jobs no one else wanted. In some ways, you may say that these empires might not have risen to such heights if it had not been for the sweat, blood, and tears of the slaves.

If one started with the first recorded evidence of slavery, they would have to follow history all the way back to ancient Sumer. It is here that archaeologists found the first mentions of laws pertaining to slaves. There, slavery existed all the way back to 2100 BCE. It seems that any empire that was built by conquering small tribes and other nations found these conquered people to be ideal for certain forms of labor. Once a tribe had been conquered, the king would sort through those remaining and choose the ones who looked the strongest, leaving the unwanted to starve and die. The ones who were chosen then were allocated to certain jobs and spent the remainder of their days serving their new masters.

No matter what region of the world an empire was in, whether the Middle East, Africa, or even the Far East, slavery became not only a necessity but also a lucrative business. However, each individual empire had different parameters and guidelines when it came to the treatment and value of slaves. Regardless, it would take a major upheaval to make any form of change.

But one thing was for sure: slavery was a booming industry and something that most either had no problem with or overlooked as if it was an everyday necessity of the time. Whether these slaves were captured in war, stolen and sold by pirates, or created through debts of their own making, there were select individuals within the populace that were nothing more than pieces of property and often treated worse than beasts of burden.

In ancient Rome, there was a large population that had found themselves being used as slave labor in all levels of society. Though there were benevolent slave owners, most slaves found their state of being to be unbearable. Eventually, like with any other empire, these less fortunate individuals would find the courage to stand up against their overlords, the Roman Republic, to win their freedom.

These wars, known as the Servile Wars, would span several decades and hundreds of miles, but none of them would quite meet the expectations of the slaves who ignited the fire of rebellion. No one in the Roman Republic would have expected that the island of Sicily would be such a hotbed for rebellion and inspire men and women to put their lives on the line for a taste of freedom. The Servile Wars were all led by charismatic and idealistic individuals who saw the pain and desire of their fellow slaves and acted upon them. Though some would eventually fall prey to that age-old corruptor of power, they would leave a mark on history.

Before diving into the historical tales, though, you have to be aware of the impact of the storytellers. There is no clear record of any of the Servile Wars, which means that the history of the wars has been told by those that either weren't there or were not part of the conflict. Though the Servile Wars left their mark on the people of that time, each of the three slave revolts made an impression on historians (both of the time and for centuries to come). The names of the heroes and villains of these stories may be the same, though; it depends on what account you are reading. For instance, if you read Diodorus of Sicily's rendition of either of the first two Servile Wars, the Sicilian slave leaders are the heroes, and the Romans are the villains. However, a Roman historian would tell a tale where the mighty Roman legions rode in to restore order to the lawless island. And the battle locations might mirror each other, but not all of the facts are so clean-cut. Depending on the historian, Spartacus could have started with four thousand or forty thousand men.

The discrepancies are due to the political leanings and nationalities of the author. So, even though these slave rebellions played a part in changing history forever, the epic tales of the battles may well be a bit skewed. In order to piece together the happenings of these wars, we have looked at multiple sources. For the first two Servile Wars, we have turned to the books of both Titus Livius (otherwise known as Livy) and Diodorus of Sicily. Both of these works, though classics in their own times, were written well after all of the slave revolts. Through the centuries, these works have been lost to wars and devastating catastrophes, so most of the tales of these heroes and villains are fragmented at best. The wars had also been altered by the decades-long game of telephone that must have gone on before the history was put down on paper.

One of the primary sources available for the Servile Wars is the *Ab Urbe Condita Libri* ("History of Rome") by Livy. This book was written between 27 BE and 9 BCE, well after the wars had ended. Thus, Livy had to depend on records and stories from people who had been told the stories by people who had heard the stories from their elders. This, of course, questions the validity of all the information in the book.

Another source that is widely used when studying these rebellions is the *Bibliotheca Historica* ("Historical Library"), written by Diodorus Siculus (Diodorus of Sicily), a Greek historian. Diodorus's book was written sometime in the 50s BCE. In order to create his text, the historian traveled the lands, gathering accounts of the historical events of each region. He also studied in Rome's archives and took note of early Roman historians' works.

The last of the most commonly studied works when it comes to the history of the Servile Wars, particularly the third and final one, is a book written by the famous Greek biographer Plutarch. In his book, *Parallel Lives* (also known as *Lives of the Noble Greeks and Romans*), he writes a compelling biography of Crassus, the man who would defeat Spartacus. The book itself is a compilation of biographies set in groups of two men, whom Plutarch compares by their virtues. Crassus was paired with the Greek Nicias (a politician with some power during the Peloponnesian War). But because of this, the biography tends to be skewed in favor of Crassus. The book was also written in the 2nd century CE, so the facts had long been manipulated, with important pieces of information being lost, no doubt, to time.

So, you can see that though historians set about to make a definitive timeline of events, they had to use information that had been altered or had huge holes. That being said, it is possible to get a basic idea of the timeline by comparing all three sources and other historical works. To make the events come to life in this book, we have decided not to stick every assumption into these pages. But even though some of the facts are uncertain, the wars were filled with heroic deeds and courageous leaders.

The Servile Wars were filled with daring military maneuverers and devastating defeats. The men and generals that fought in them would find their names forever etched in the annals of time. Some would be immortalized as heroic figures who stood up for their fellow men, and others would be villainized for their presumption that slaves could possibly be on the same level as Roman citizens. Even though the history books may not be wholly accurate, these uprisings caused the wheels of change to begin turning in the mighty Roman Republic and the future Roman Empire.

Chapter 1 – Slavery in Rome

Understanding the atmosphere that bred the three uprisings means diving deep into slavery and the world of the Roman Republic. The Roman Republic spread over most of Europe, and in order to be able to maintain this growth, a large majority of the population was relegated to slave labor. These individuals had no dominion over themselves and were used in a wide range of industries and jobs. From simple household chores to working in the mines, these men and women (and children too) were used to ensure that those tasks that were too manually intensive and undesirable for Roman citizens got done.

Though, in our modern world, slavery is frowned upon, it was a natural and everyday occurrence that most Romans believed to be a necessity. Not only was this accepted as a societal norm, but it was also a religious and philosophical one as well. The concept of slavery and complete control over an individual was present in Roman mythology and Roman philosophy, both of which also stressed the inability for freedom without some sort of indentured servitude. As the Roman Republic expanded and more and more principalities and countries fell to them, many of the conquered populations became slaves.

Of course, not everyone was fit to become a slave. Those who had no skill to work manual labor jobs found themselves at the end of a sword. With 20 percent of the Roman Republic populace being slaves (this number, of course, ebbed and flowed with the expansion of the republic), one may wonder how the number got so high. As the republic expanded and wars were fought and won, many of the fallen enemies of the republic were taken captive and eventually sold into slavery. Not only soldiers were drafted into slavery. Those of lower social standing who had no skills to offer were also targeted. These types of slaves wound up being moved from the area they were taken to different parts of the country or even sent abroad on slave vessels to be sold in other markets.

But along with this, there was also piracy, as well as debt collection and condemnation for a crime. Civil offenses like theft would be heard during a private trial, and it was possible that the person convicted of the crime could be forced into servitude until the value of the goods that had been stolen was repaid. For those who committed a grave civil offense, they could actually end up in a life of slavery.

For those individuals who found themselves living as slaves, the desire to have a family didn't subside. Those individuals would inevitably find themselves with children, and these children were thus born into slavery.

Because of the expansion of the Roman Republic, those of noble status or who had immense lands found the need for more laborers. The influx of slaves from these regions, as well as from other means, had a huge impact on the economy, as they left the economy dependent on slavery. No matter what large city one went to in the Roman Republic, there was no doubt they would find a large slave market where men, women, and children were bought and sold like cattle. Many ports along the Mediterranean were more known for their slave markets than their actual markets.

A large number of slaves came to the shores of Italy through these markets, where they were purchased by the Roman elites. To fill these markets up, many slave traders would follow in the wake of the Roman military forces and acquire people to sell. The slave traders looked for strong men and sometimes children who could grow into strong men. Then they would take them back and sell them via public auctions or even individually to elite buyers.

The slave traders would place these slaves on display for sale in several ways. Some traders did this by putting people on revolving stages, where the slaves would have a sign around their neck with several important attributes, including where they were from and their education. The price of the slave would be determined via their age, their quality, and skills. In order to ensure that the buyers were aware of what they were buying, these slaves were put on display without any clothes. This process was overseen by low-level Roman officials.

After a while, it was clear that the influx of slaves both from the Roman conquests as well as the plethora of other sources could be beneficial to the government. This led to an eventual sales tax being placed on slaves. It originally started at 2 percent under the rule of Augustus, and eventually, by 43 CE, it worked its way up to 4 percent.

Because of the common feelings among society when it came to slaves, these poor individuals found themselves at the bottom of the barrel, with even criminals being more a citizen of the republic than them. This fact alone shows how little thought was given to the treatment and legal status of slaves in the Roman Republic.

There were many concepts and philosophies being formed during this important period in history. One of the most common was that the role of an individual was synonymous with who they were. This translated into most Roman citizens believing that a slave was not a person at all. After all, these slaves were not owners of their own bodies, lacked ancestral lineage, and tended to have no name.

This also translated into a lot of different laws being put in place in regard to slaves. For instance, a slave could not testify in any court case unless there had been bodily harm done to them by the individual. In fact, Roman slaves had very little rights whatsoever for most of the year and found themselves doing the jobs that the Roman elite couldn't be bothered with. However, the slaves could enjoy the festival of Saturnalia, which was the one day of the year where they were permitted to set down their tools and join their masters in celebration. But the next day, no matter what condition they were in, it was back to work for them.

Many slaves found themselves working multiple different jobs throughout the year, depending on the season. It was very common for a slave to work in the fields during harvest season and then to find themselves in the servitude of private homes for the remainder of the year. The main five divisions of jobs that slaves were acquired to do were domestic, public, urban works and services, farming, and mining. Their jobs would be further broken down into specific work within these fields.

How the slaves lived would depend on what type of job they were purchased to do. For those who were brought into a Roman elite's or noble's home, their living spaces were often much more comfortable and elaborate than those who lived in a tradesman's home. Though they didn't have a comfortable life by any stretch of the imagination, many of the Roman elite household slaves had their own quarters and modest clothing. After all, the number of slaves a person had was a sign of their standing in society, and being able to clothe and house numerous slaves would reflect well on them.

On the other hand, those who were chosen to work in the mines and quarries lived out their days doing strenuous manual labor and living in hovels. If a person wound up being purchased by a gladiator school or a nobleman who wanted his own gladiator, they would have a unique life that could possibly be both full of fame and torture. Another form of employment that was open to slaves was that of a servus publicus. These slaves were not privately owned but were rather owned by the public in general. Most of these slaves wound up doing work in temples and colleges. This gave them a unique life, just like the slaves who found their way into gladiator schools. Many of these slaves would gain some education, and that would give them a pretty big advantage when it came to possibly gaining their freedom. There were even some slaves who were able to build a reputation for themselves and do more skilled work, as well as earn money. Many times, this type of slave could work their way into manumission more easily than other slaves.

The intensive labor that the slaves of the Roman Republic endured was backbreaking and exhausting, but there was the ability for some slaves to claim freedom. Manumission, in essence, means that slaves were either freed by their owners or had worked off their debt, thereby earning their freedom. Unlike Greece, Rome treated freed slaves in a much more compassionate manner. After manumission (the act of a master freeing a slave), these men and women could work their way into becoming a citizen of the republic. Manumission was done in full view of the public and was overseen by a public official to make it legal. The master looking to release the slave would use a staff and touch it to the slave's head to proclaim the slave's freedom. After this ceremony had been performed, the slave was then given a felt cap to wear as a sign that they had been freed.

Manumission allowed slaves the opportunity to own property, as well as to participate in government, that is, as long as they were born a male. These former slaves fell into the social class known as the libertini. Although they could vote and accumulate wealth, they were unable to run for any office. Still, freed slaves had the ability to gain influence even without having any type of official power.

The process of building one's reputation was lengthy and included a period of time where their previous master became their patron. The arrangement left the master and now freed slave with a list of obligations that had to be completed before the slave was truly free. Along with this, any child born after a slave had been freed would be born a citizen with full rights. The process of manumission was very difficult and very rare, but there are documents and stories about slaves who were able to do this. However, for the majority of slaves, this was not an option.

Roman masters saw their slaves as nothing more than property, and this left them with the ability to treat their slaves as they saw fit. That meant that many slaves lived in squalor and harsh environments, which broke not only their bodies but also their spirits. Living in this fashion ravaged many and led to numerous deaths. However, it would also lead to several individuals standing up from the crowd and inspiring their fellow slaves to stand with them. These leaders of the beaten-down masses of the slave class would look to make some impact on the world they lived in. The first of these individuals would ignite a fire on the island of Sicily in 135 BCE.

Chapter 2 – The Foundations of Rebellion (Or a Brief History of the Island of Sicily)

Pressure had been building for decades on the little island of Sicily. Rebellions like the ones that made up the first two Servile Wars weren't just born; they were cultivated, and they started in 900 BCE. The native Sicilians, who consisted of multiple small tribes, had been trading with the mighty Phoenician Empire for quite some time. Eventually, the Phoenicians decided it would be best to set up trading posts to cement their partnership with these native tribes. It also had the added benefit of making their presence felt at all times. Not needing to go much farther inland than the coast, the Phoenicians left a majority of the island open for other nations to settle. This would be one of the many catalysts that left the island ripe for rebellion in 135 BCE.

In 750 BCE, the first of these other nations would land when Greek ships sailed into the harbors on the western side of the island. For centuries, this division of the island seemed to work just fine, but eventually, the Phoenician posts would be enveloped into the Carthaginian hegemony. As the Greeks continued expanding throughout the Mediterranean, the Magonid dynasty stepped up to stop that expansion, and the Carthaginian hegemony was born. This union would be the spark that ignited several flames of rebellion, which would lead to centuries of dissent and bloody battles. In regards to Sicily, the Phoenicians joined the battle and formed an alliance with one of the native tribes to keep the encroaching Greeks from taking their part of the island.

The Greek settlements on the island managed their business just like those on the southern shores of Italy itself and Greece. But even amongst them, there was tension. The island of Sicily had been settled by two factions: the Ionians and the Dorians. The Ionians maintained a good relationship with the Sicilians and the Phoenicians. However, the Dorians were not nearly as friendly and wanted nothing more than to expand their territory, even if it meant taking land from the Phoenicians and the native Sicilians. Of course, the trade routes and naval capabilities allowed all of these factions to become quite wealthy, which, in turn, allowed the more expansion-minded Dorian Greeks to begin increasing their territories.

By 540 BCE, the Carthaginians had worked their way into control of Sicily. Though there were minor skirmishes, for the most part, the Greeks and Carthaginians seemed to reside in peace during this period of time; that is, until a Spartan prince named Dorieus lost his throne, took his people, and sailed west. He found his way to Sicily, where he asserted his authority and expanded Greek trade and territory. After the passing of Dorieus, the excommunicated Spartan king broke ties and left the Greeks on Sicily on their own. This, of course, meant that those Greeks with power began to seize even more influence.

These power-hungry Greeks turned rapidly into tyrants, with a few of those gaining superior power and ruling the island with an iron fist. Though there was still a division amongst the Greeks along Ionian and Dorian lines, the Dorian Greeks eventually began to overtake the Ionians. Under this rule, the Greek tyrants began a process of removing all the Ionians from their cities through deportation and enslavement, as well as ethnic cleansing. Political moves and alliances were the only cards the Ionians had up their sleeves, but eventually, they needed to reach out for help from their more powerful allies, the Carthaginians, which would begin the First Sicilian War.

When the Persians attacked Greece in 480 BCE, the Carthaginians felt it was the perfect time to make a move on the island, and they did so with the largest Carthaginian military force ever put together. This massive undertaking quickly took care of Theron, one of the Greek tyrants who had seized control of the island. But even with this victory, there was still quite the fight ahead for the Carthaginians before they could call Sicily theirs.

After months of fighting, the Carthaginians were met by Gelo at Himera, which would be the last battle of the conflict. Prince Gelo would ride out of Syracuse, where his father, King Hiero II, sat on the throne, to stop the Carthaginians from moving farther into Sicily. The conflict at Himera would be a bloody battle that would cost many men their lives. The mighty Carthaginian King Hamilcar was mortally wounded during the battle, and the Carthaginians retreated in defeat. Though there was no loss of land on either side, the reparations and the funds secured from the war allowed the Greek presence to flourish.

For seventy years, there was a delicate balance when it came to power on the island. While this peace was maintained, the Carthaginian Empire expanded, encroaching on lands ranging from North Africa to the Iberian Peninsula. In 416 BCE, the peace between the Dorian Geeks and the Ionian Greeks was shattered when the cities of Selinus and Segesta reignited their feud. Like in the previous conflict, the Ionians fell back on relying on their allies for help, but this time, the Carthaginians ignored their pleas. But the Ionians were not left alone, as the Greeks heard their call and responded by sending reinforcements. This, of course, caught the attention of the Carthaginians, and they soon rethought their original stance and joined the battle. However, they wanted to solve the problems with diplomacy. In order to do that, though, they had to bring the Sicilians and Greeks to the table, and the only way to do that was through force.

Diplomacy would be intermixed with battles, and eventually, the Carthaginians would gain control over Sicily and begin the height of their reign. Over the next three centuries, there would be five more Sicilian Wars until Rome finally got involved seriously, causing the first of the Punic Wars to begin. Rome and Carthage would struggle for control over the island, with the Carthaginians and Romans ending up at the negotiating table. Rome would annex Sicily, and because Carthage was the defeated party, it would also have to pay reparations. This, however, was not the last time these two mighty empires would come up against each other in Sicily.

In 215 BCE, a rivalry was sparked by Hannibal's push into Roman territories, one of which was Sicily. For several years, conflicts would rage until the Carthaginian forces were toppled by the Roman forces and the plague. Having taken a hit from all sides, the Carthaginians packed up and went home, leaving the island to the Romans. This rapid departure changed a lot of things on the island, and the biggest of all was the idea of owning land. Romans from the mainland sought to capture some of the prime lands that were now available at bargain prices. For those Sicilians who had supported Carthage and still held tracts of land, they would soon find themselves at the mercy of Roman executioners. In the end, the Sicilians who were left on the island that had been Greek or Roman supporters, together with the Sicilians and Greeks from the mainland, were able to swallow up all the land.

These new landowners had a different mentality when it came to the slave population on the island. With most of them being there as part of the reparations or from other places like Macedonia and other parts of the Mediterranean, the elite had little empathy or sympathy for the slaves. The new landowners' attitudes led to many of them treating their slaves more poorly than normal. Under the influence of power, these men turned to savagery, like starving their slaves and leaving them exposed to the elements by not providing the right clothes for them. An influx of slaves from pirates and the corruption of the Roman governors would lead to even more inhumane behavior.

On top of the squalid conditions that the slaves of Sicily had to put up with, there were elite members of Roman society who found ways to entertain themselves. However, this would cost many slaves their lives. One type of entertainment included setting up manhunts on select estates, where slaves were the prey for these barbarous Roman men. After all, these socialites had an ample supply of slaves steadily coming to their shores, so it was financially beneficial to work their slaves to the bone and simply replace them than it would be to build shelters and make sure they had all the necessities in order to survive.

The poor treatment of these slaves led them to turn to crime in order to make sure they and their families were fed and clothed. Because of the isolation of the island itself, the Romans paid little attention to what was actually going on there. This left the corrupt Roman governors on the island to oversee the situation, and Sicily soon became known as a dangerous destination and a place where one's life was constantly in peril. This atmosphere and the treatment of the slaves would lead to two slaves marshaling their comrades together and rising up against the Sicilian Roman slave owners in 135 BCE. Though these two men would stand up on their own, they would eventually join together and form an alliance that would withstand the Roman onslaught for several years.

Chapter 3 – Eunus and His Prophecy

It was challenging for a slave to elevate their worth in the eyes of their owners. But amongst the slaves of the Sicilian Greek Antigenes was one who was able to do just that. Eunus was born in Syria, and he had a special power that his owner loved to trot out in front of his friends and special dignitaries. Eunus was thought to have the sight, as he was supposedly able to conjure magic and prophesize. (However, some scholars in later years would refute this, saying he was able to command attention due to his charisma.) Many nights, this slave would regale his owner and others with his prophecies and tricks for hours on end. Eunus would do everything from making things disappear and reappear to breathing fire. One of his many tricks was to tell tales and prophecies.

One particular night, he began talking of a future where the Sicilian upper class would feel the pain of the people they abused every day. In his prophecy, Eunus described in detail how the slaves would rise up and topple their rulers and how the upper class would either be killed or enslaved. These slaves would turn to him for leadership, and he would end up on the throne. Most of the slave owners found this quite humorous, and some even gave him tips for this wild tale. Those who opted to award him for his words made a vow that if he ever sat on the throne, they would be safe from both death and enslavement.

Word of Eunus's prophecies soon found their way to the slaves, and in desperation, the slaves reached out for guidance. Like many others, the slaves of Damophilus, a wealthy landowner who dealt out excessively harsh treatment, had had enough. So, a group of them snuck out and found their way to Eunus. Once they found him, they began telling their tales of mistreatment, including being branded and other horrendous torture. They even went on to discuss that the torture was done not only by the head of the household but also by his evil wife.

After listening to their story and being asked what he thought they should do, Eunus responded the only way he could. He informed these beaten-down men that it had come time for his prophecy to become a reality. Eunus told them that the gods were on their side and that they should gather together with other slaves and follow him to Enna, which would be their first victory on the road to overthrowing their cruel masters. When the slaves returned to Eunus, they no longer were just a handful of men. Instead, they now numbered somewhere near four hundred strong.

Amassed before their leader, they pledged their allegiance to him, and they then armed themselves with what they could find. Full of rage, which was specifically aimed at their master, the slaves were spurred on by the encouraging words of Eunus. The slaves were now ready to take the pivotal city of Enna. The city itself was easily taken, as no one suspected this type of attack could have been possible. The slaves mercilessly left few people without a mark. Of those, the fact that they chose to spare the ironsmiths was perhaps the most vital move to the uprising's success. Keeping them alive and their forges intact would allow the slave army to replenish their weapons more easily.

But that wasn't what they had come for, and so, the slaves ripped through the houses of the city, dragging the owners and their families into the street and committing unthinkable atrocities. No one was safe in this rage-filled bloodbath, not even the children. There were accounts of the slaves ripping children from their parent's arms and tossing them viciously to the ground. (This was, of course, written in the history annals of a later time, so no one can be sure if this actually happened; if it did, it was certainly brutal.) The slave army saved the worst atrocities for their owners and the other elites in the city, though. As the slaves ran through the streets, more slaves joined in, creating even more chaos.

As the slaves finished pillaging the city, word reached them that the man who had ignited this flame was holed up outside of the city with his family. This was unacceptable, so the slaves sent a group to collect Damophilus and his family and bring them back into the city to receive their punishment. It took very little effort to overcome Damophilus and his relations. The barbaric master and his wife were tied up. The benevolent daughter of Damophilus was spared by the slaves, as she had always been kind to them. The leader of the mob appointed several men to take the young woman to Catana (modern-day Catania), where she would be placed in the care of relatives. Once she was off on her journey, her parents were driven down the roads and into the city, with insults being hurled at them on their way.

The couple was pulled by their bindings through the streets of Enna and soon found themselves standing in the middle of the theater surrounded by angry eyes and bitter words. Damophilus quickly began to plead with the slaves, using his fine skills of oration. His words began to reach the crowds, calming their fears and turning the tide of opinion. But for those slaves he was cruelest to, they didn't want to wait for the verdict of the masses. They knew they would not get what they wanted, so they took action. Two of his slaves stepped forward, and one of them pierced his chest with a sword while the other swung his ax at his neck. The crowd was startled, but that soon disappeared as a wave of joy swept over them upon realizing that they had succeeded in taking Enna and were now well on their way to freedom.

Seeing that the slaves were all looking at him, Eunus took to the stage and was soon voted in as king. His prophecy had been fulfilled, and it didn't take him long to begin making decrees. Eunus's first action as king was to rename himself, and he chose a powerful name from his Syrian ancestry. He would henceforth be known as King Antiochus. He then called to his people and bade them bring the prisoners forward and ordered them all to be executed except for the wife of Damophilus and the new king's own masters. Damophilus's wife had a fate worse than death. King Antiochus decreed that she would now be the property of the female slaves she had brutally tormented. The female slaves tortured her for a while, and when they tired of it, they sent the woman over a cliff to her death. As for Eunus's owners, he took pride and enjoyment by taking their lives with his own hands.

After all that was taken care of, it was now time for King Antiochus to finish his coronation. He took fine clothing for himself from the homes of the now-deceased upper class of Enna and found a crown as well. Now that he looked the part, he needed a queen, and for this, he turned to the woman who had traveled with him and had been his living companion, making her his consort. King Antiochus then took the men from amongst the mob who had shown some insight and intelligence and created a council to advise him. With all of this now in place, he was ready to continue his rebellion and build a kingdom in which the slaves of Sicily would rule over the Romans, Greeks, and Carthaginians who still resided on the island.

Chapter 4 – The First Servile War

King Antiochus and his slave rebellion was an inspiration to the other slaves on the island, and it didn't take long for a large uprising to begin. In fact, on the southern part of the island, a Roman slave named Cleon would amass a slave army as no one had ever seen. Cleon had found his way to Sicily after being taken captive in his homeland of Cilicia, which can be found in the southeastern region of modern-day Turkey. Because of the poor treatment by his master, Cleon resorted to theft and murder. Cleon had had enough, and he was encouraged by the capture of Enna to reach out to his fellow slaves in the area. It didn't take long before he had gathered somewhere in the area of five thousand men. With his army amassed, Cleon set his sights on taking Agrigentum. The city fell without much effort, just like Enna.

The Romans on the mainland and on the island itself now began to take notice. However, they still didn't have any ideas on how to combat the new problem; they actually thought the two rival slave armies would eventually turn on each other. Unfortunately, this was not to be, as Eunus reached out to Cleon, and the two merged their forces. Cleon proudly stepped into the position of general under the new king. It wasn't long before King Antiochus's army went from a mere 10,000 soldiers to 200,000, at least according to some accounts. With this massive army, the Roman leadership began to worry and take note. In order to nip this insurrection in the bud, the Roman leadership sent one of their generals to the island as a governor, and he was backed up by eight thousand soldiers.

Lucius Hypsaeus was the first in a long line of praetors sent by the Roman Senate that looked to squash this slave rebellion with ease. But they all were greeted with a mounting army and men who fought for a cause and knew the lands well. Unfortunately, this combination was too deadly, and praetor after praetor failed to get the job done. The unsuccessful campaigns against King Antiochus even spurred slaves in the capital city itself to attempt a revolt; however, this small conclave of slaves failed. This minor disruption gained even more ire from the Roman Senate, though, and in 133 BCE, the mighty praetor Lucius Calpurnius Piso was tasked with the job of ridding Rome of this nuisance.

Piso struggled like the other praetors at first but not in the same way. After being given this duty, he began forming an army that could face King Antiochus's army. But this proved to be challenging, as the Roman citizens had turned against the concept of conscription, and none of the lower classes had any property, which didn't give them an incentive to fight for anything. Eventually, after a lot of hard work, the praetor was able to amass a decent-sized force of soldiers, and they set off for the shores of Sicily. The Roman forces landed in the port city of Messana (modern-day Messina), where they were unsure of how they would be received.

To the praetor's surprise, the people of the city met the Roman legion with open arms. The Roman Senate had hopes that Lucius Calpurnius Piso could take the city without bloodshed, and the senators sent Piso with a decree that gave the city an exemption when it came to levies and taxes on their property. But though the people in the city seemed willing to take this gift and move on, King

Antiochus heard of the landing, and he moved his troops toward the city, ready for combat.

Thus, before the city of Messana could be officially taken, Lucius Calpurnius Piso and his legion had to confront the slave army. The two forces met on the battlefield just outside of Messana at Kurkourakis (modern-day Curcuraci). But King Antiochus had underestimated the Roman forces, and the slave army retreated, leaving eight thousand slaves behind as captives of the Roman legion. In order to send a message to King Antiochus and the people of Messana, Piso took those eight thousand slaves and executed them, hanging them in open view of whoever dared to pass by the blood-soaked battlefield. Once these rebels had been taken care of, the praetor moved his legion toward the walled city of Tauromenium (present-day Taormina).

The Roman legion marched to the city of Naxos and then surmounted the hill where Tauromenium sat, planning to lay siege to the mighty citadel. The city, however, was protected by a large contingent from King Antiochus's army, so the Roman legion found this task quite difficult. It seemed that Komanus, the leader of the Sicilian slave army in this outpost and Cleon's brother, was well versed in military tactics, and that, coupled with the well-built defenses of the city, made Tauromenium unbreachable. Fearing that this siege would take too long and cost too much, Piso and his legion retreated and refocused their attention on Morgantina and Enna. (Morgantina was another major city on the island.)

The terrain was treacherous, as the Roman legion led by the confident praetor found itself going west through the remnants of the mighty Mount Etna. But the landscape also worked in their favor, as they found themselves going toward Morgantina through the canyon that housed the Alcantara River. This gave them easy access to water and a definite focal point to watch for potential attacks from King Antiochus's troops. The march to Morgantina took several days, but eventually, the city came into view, and Piso's legions set up for another siege.

Unlike Tauromenium, Morgantina fell pretty quickly. Lucius Piso and his legion were able to break the city, and they took the remaining men of the rebel slave army and crucified them for everyone to see the consequences for standing up against the mighty Roman Republic. With another of King Antiochus's fortresses taken, Piso continued his conquest to reclaim Sicily for Rome. Next up on his agenda was the citadel of Antiochus's power—Enna.

Marching north, Lucius Calpurnius Piso found a strategic location at the bottom of the hill where Enna stood. He set his troops up to once again lay a siege. The Roman general took advantage of the massive flat landscape there and rolled his catapults forward. For days, the Roman forces sent heavy boulders and anything they could get into their catapults to bombard the city.

Peppered throughout the heavy bombardment were many skirmishes, but the Roman forces just couldn't break Antiochus or his troops. Eventually, the slave army was able to deal a death blow to Piso's siege. During a skirmish with one of the Roman leader's cavalry units, the slave army was able to surround the Romans, forcing them to surrender. With this defeat, the Roman forces lost not only men and weapons but also horses. This infuriated the Roman general, and he dealt the leader of the cavalry and the remaining men who returned to the camp a humiliating punishment. The men were relegated to the lowest ranks of the army, and as for the head of the cavalry unit, he was made to stand as Piso's tent guard clothed in rags. He was also not allowed to bathe or wear shoes. Hoping this would inspire fear of failure, Piso made it a point to ridicule the cavalry leader at every turn. But even with his punishment (which did not inspire the fear Piso had hoped) and determination, Enna was impregnable.

Lucius Calpurnius Piso returned to Rome after a year of conquest to stand before the Senate. Though he had some successes, he had to stand in front of his leaders and admit that his campaign had been unsuccessful. Fending off attacks on all sides, the Senate knew that they had to squash the issues on Sicily so they could utilize these forces in other parts of the republic. For instance, they could use those men to shore up their borders in places like Spain, which had been dealing with the Celtiberian uprising. So, the Senate continued sending praetor after praetor in order to remove Antiochus from his throne and regain control of Sicily.

In 133 BCE, the parade of praetors continued with Marcus Perperna. Like his predecessors, Marcus Perperna knew that the answer to toppling Antiochus's regime was to take Enna. So, after his legion landed on Sicily, he immediately began marching toward the citadel. As the Roman praetor's troops neared Enna, they came upon a camp of Antiochus's troops. Knowing that the slave army would have to pass through them and not wanting to have any forces coming to the citadel's aid, Marcus Perperna opted to surround these troops and battle them. The conflict took quite a bit of time, but King Antiochus's troops, starving and riddled with plague, had no choice but to surrender. The Roman leader wanted to send a message to Antiochus, and like the praetors before him, he thought crucifying the remaining enemy soldiers was the way to do that.

Unfortunately, this defeat and subsequent display of power didn't have the desired effect, and Marcus Perperna had to return to Rome with this lackluster victory. After all, this was just one squadron of Antiochus's soldiers, and with their defeat, most of the king's army flocked to his side to protect him and their capital. But the victory was a sign that the Roman forces would defeat Antiochus's entrenched forces, so when Marcus Perperna returned to Rome, he was greeted with a hero's welcome. Knowing that Rome was busy celebrating their meager win, Antiochus ordered

Cleon to move on Messana, the main point of access for the Roman troops from the mainland.

Wanting to eliminate the Roman legions' access point, Antiochus's forces moved on Messana, overtaking a large swath of the city, including the fortress and the harbor. The bulk of the city's population was able to find shelter behind the walls, saving themselves from horrible deaths. However, the fortress was quickly fortified, and the harbor was blocked with a chain so that the Roman forces were unable to enter without scuttling their ships. With the taking of Messana, Antiochus's kingdom ranged from the southern coastal region of the island all the way to the eastern coast, leaving very little land still controlled by Roman allies or forces. With these new developments, the Roman Senate had had it with this slave king and his rebels. With this sentiment prevalent in the Senate, they passionately pled with the consuls to play their part and help get rid of the problem.

Of course, the Senate felt they should retake the port city they had just lost, and the consuls that met with the Senate agreed. Two very well-known individuals in Roman politics took up the challenge of overthrowing the slave king. Publius Rupilius and Publius Popilius Laenas were members of a committee that had meted out justice in a recent assassination of a major Roman political figure, and they had built quite the reputation for their fervent love of the republic. Though both were not well known when it came to their military capabilities, as part of the committee, they had garnered many honors, which the two would use to build an army to meet Antiochus's troops on the battlefield. Once the legions had been enlisted, Rupilius and Laenas began their long march south.

Rupilius and Laenas arrived on the Calabrian coast just across the Strait of Messina, but word of their pending arrival had already found its way to the court of Antiochus. In order to combat these Roman legions, Antiochus ordered Cleon to disperse squadrons of their army along the northern coast. Unfortunately, though,

Antiochus's troops didn't quite make it far enough north, as the Roman legions of Laenas and Rupilius had already sailed across the strait and found a good base camp in the large inlet known as Paradise Bay. Once Rupilius and Laenas were securely situated in the inlet, they constructed a strategic plan that would utilize the fact they were better equipped than their enemies.

The two consuls separated their fleet into smaller fleets, and these were sent into the harbor of Messana for days on end. This, of course, put pressure on the defensive forces of Antiochus's troops, as it did not allow them any time to recoup after the attacks. Rupilius watched the battles from his ship in Paradise Bay, waiting for the pressure to be too much that it would leave a crack in Messana's defenses. Eventually, his fleet's constant bombardment of the city did just that, and it was time for a land attack. After marshaling his troops, Rupilius pushed his fleet into the harbor, making landfall with his mighty legion.

The days of assault gave the Roman legion the upper hand, and with a bloody push into the city, the forces of Antiochus were overthrown. The streets were strewn with bodies, and there would be many more, as Rupilius was able to take eight thousand slaves as hostages. Rupilius waited for the major part of the battle to be done before he, too, made landfall and continued the savagery. In order to make his victory evident and let the king of the slaves know that he was on his way to him, Rupilius took those eight thousand slaves and nailed them to crosses as he traveled along the coast from Messana to Capo Peloro, leaving them to suffer in the sun. Some died immediately, while others would take days to die. Either way, the message was clear: Rupilius intended to be the one to end this rebellion and return Sicily to Rome.

Rupilius moved toward Tauromenium, taking his legion along the coast. This would be his next big hurdle, as this city was fortified with well-built walls and a legion of Antiochus's men, which was led by Cleon's brother, Komanus. In an effort to have a peaceful surrender, Rupilius offered the city's leaders the chance to surrender, but they were too devoted to their king and their freedom, so they refused. Having no other recourse, Rupilius had his troops dig in for a siege. The Roman forces surrounded the city for days, and with each passing day, the people inside faced dwindling supplies until they could no longer take it. They sent a representative to Rupilius to talk about conditions for a peaceful solution. Rupilius now knew that his plan was working, so he sent the courier back with the answer that nothing short of unconditional surrender would bring his tortuous siege to an end.

This answer was not even an option for the besieged forces within the city. Though there had been rumors of cannibalism and there were sick people everywhere in the city, the former slaves could not see dying any other way than as freemen. Unfortunately for Antiochus's forces in the city, there were those who were perfectly comfortable with the terms. One of the slaves, Sarapion, found his way to the Roman camp and quickly revealed everything that Rupilius needed to break the defenses of Komanus and his troops in the hopes he might be spared.

With this knowledge, Rupilius spurred his legion into action. The strategy was simple: the infantry would charge the walls, using their shields to protect them from the projectiles of their enemies as well as their own forces. Behind these infantrymen, Rupilius instructed his archers and catapults to bombard the city. This tactic put extreme pressure on Antiochus's troops inside the fortress, and eventually, the Roman legions broke through the citadel's defenses. As the legions tore through the streets, Komanus realized all was lost. In an effort to save himself from the fate that awaited him if he was taken hostage, Komanus chose to take his own life.

Rupilius and his troops took the city quickly and once again found themselves in possession of hundreds of captives. These prisoners were tired and hungry, but the end of the siege was not the end of their suffering. Just like he did in Messana, Rupilius wanted to send a message. At Tauromenium, this meant torture and a ghastly end for the prisoners. Once the soldiers and Rupilius were done tormenting their captives, the soldiers marched them to the top of the city's walls and herded them over the edge to their deaths.

Rupilius also found that he had done the impossible—he had captured Antiochus himself. After the city fell, one of the soldiers stumbled upon a pit with a slave hiding inside. The soldier dragged the slave from the pit, and the man was brought in front of Rupilius, who quickly realized who the man was. Knowing that the end of the revolt was near, he sent Antiochus to Morgantina to await punishment. He would not make it to his judgment, though, as the slave king would fall sick and die waiting for his trial.

The rebellion wasn't quite done yet. Rupilius knew he had to take Enna before he could claim utter victory over the slave rebellion. Cleon had barricaded himself in the city's walls, waiting for the impending battle. As Rupilius lined his legion up outside the city's walls, Cleon felt the only way to save himself and his troops was to charge the line. Thinking he could break the lines and flee to safety, he urged his troops out onto the field. Cleon would not find his way to freedom, though; rather, he would perish due to wounds sustained during the conflict.

Without their leader, the rebel troops and the city of Enna fell to Rupilius with ease. The slave army crumbled, and Sicily was once again under Roman control. Once again, Rupilius utilized his captives to deter the slaves left on the island from thinking about ever doing something like this again. Rupilius took over twenty thousand prisoners of war and crucified them as he moved his legions to the coast. He and his legions returned to Rome in victory, and the First Servile War came to an end after three years and thousands of lost lives. But though the war had ended in favor of Rome, the slaves' memories and sentiments of the rebellion in

Sicily never wavered. It was just a matter of time before that rebellious spirit was ignited once again.

Chapter 5 – The Cimbrian War: Catalyst for the Second Servile War

It had been twenty-three years since the uprising of the slaves in Sicily had troubled the Roman government. In that time, the Roman Republic had expanded and became a mighty power in the Mediterranean. It seemed that nobody would be able to stop the growth of this powerful empire. But in 113 BCE, the ever-growing Roman Republic would be challenged by a large Germanic horde from the north, which began to migrate into the northern parts of Europe. The migration had actually started two years earlier when the Cimbri began their long southward trek from the Jutland peninsula.

Due to harsh winters and continual flooding of the lands they called home, the Cimbri knew that they had to find a new place to settle, and mainland Europe seemed to be perfect for them. So, the tribe packed up their belongings, and men, women, and children began their long search for a new homeland. As they made the long journey, their numbers began to increase, as hundreds of thousands of people from other tribes (the Ambrones and Teutones, to be specific) joined them in search of a new home. These other tribes were suffering from the same issues that the Cimbri had, and they desperately needed to find a new homeland as well.

In 113 BCE, this caravan had worked its way south and reached Noricum, which was ruled over by the Taurisci. This kingdom, which was located in the northern parts of the Alps, had been ruled by the federation of Celtic tribes for quite a while. But as they looked out and saw the huge masses of Germanic tribes moving toward them, they knew that they were no match for the sheer number of warriors housed within those ranks. Understanding this, the Celtic chief sent word to his ally in the south, which was none other than Rome. Not wanting this Germanic horde to make its way closer to Rome, the Roman Senate agreed to help and soon sent a Roman consul named Gnaeus Carbo to help with the problem.

Carbo, like many other Roman consuls, looked to have his name etched in history and to build his reputation amongst his fellow Roman patricians. With this in mind, he marched his legion into the Celtic tribal lands and set up camp at a strategic point. Knowing that he would have the upper hand, Carbo was shocked when emissaries from the Germanic tribes appeared before him in his tent. The Cimbri had heard through their travels south of the power of the Roman Republic, and they didn't want to end up in a conflict with them. Instead, they approached the Roman consul and bartered for a peace treaty. Carbo only delivered one condition for the treaty, and that was that the Germanic tribes would immediately leave the Celtic territory. The Cimbri complied with this.

Though Carbo had agreed upon a tentative peace treaty, he did not intend to honor this treaty. The Cimbri packed up their people and were escorted by a handful of Roman soldiers from the Celtic lands. However, the Roman soldiers who were given the task to escort the Germanic tribes were also instructed to guide them into an ambush. Unfortunately for Carbo, one of the guides did not want to cause harm to the women and children, and he betrayed the Roman consul.

So, as Carbo's men led the Germanic tribes into what was to be an ambush, he and his men soon found themselves descended upon by thousands of Germanic warriors. In an effort to prove their military might, the Germanic warriors mercilessly killed almost every Roman soldier, but Carbo and a handful of his soldiers were able to escape. Upon returning home, Carbo found that he was to be prosecuted because of his failure. The trial was short and ended with the verdict that he should be exiled. To save face, Carbo took his own life rather than be separated from his beloved Rome.

Rome was now on high alert and prepared itself for more conflicts with this rampaging German horde. The Cimbri and their Germanic brethren continued looking for lands they could settle and make their own. As they moved west into the Gallic lands, they razed and pillaged many different territories. As they did this, many Gallic tribes chose to join them rather than resist. This meant that the threat to Rome was growing larger and looming closer and closer to the center of Roman power. This was unacceptable, and Rome soon began sending legions to combat the Germanic tribes and to bolster the forces of their allies throughout southern Gaul.

The Cimbri horde and its victories over Roman allies and Roman legions empowered smaller tribes in the area. Tribes such as the Helvetti moved against Roman troops stationed in the area of Tolosa. This incursion caused the Roman proconsul (a governor of a province) in charge of the area to mobilize his troops to regain the city. After the victory, Quintus Servilius Caepio, the proconsul, feared that the Cimbri would eventually turn their attention to Rome, so he developed a defensive strategy and waited for the inevitable push toward Roman territories. It didn't take long for the united Germanic tribes to do just that. While the forces moved closer and closer to Rome itself, the Senate opted to move legions north to fortify Caepio's position.

Uncharacteristically, though, the Roman Senate opted to send an untried and inexperienced military leader to do the job: Gnaeus Mallius Maximus. This strategic miscalculation would eventually lead to a devastating loss. The two proconsuls set up camp along both banks of the Rhone River near the Roman city of Arausio, and they both jockeyed for control of the legions. Technically, though, Gnaeus Mallius Maximus had seniority over Quintus Servilius Caepio, but Caepio would not bow down to Mallius's control. Because of this, the battle would be carried out as a two-pronged attack, dividing the forces and leaving them open to disaster.

Mallius sent a picketing group forward, headed by the legate Marcus Aurelius Scaurus, in order to have enough warning of a potential Cimbrian attack. But this small force wasn't enough to withstand the sheer number of Cimbrian warriors who attacked them. Most of the Roman troops of the picketing line were killed. The legate and a few of his soldiers were captured, and they were brought to the king of the Cimbri, Boiorix. Maintaining the Roman bravado, Scaurus stood before the Germanic king and offered to allow the Germanic tribes to retreat from the land or face the consequences of choosing to fight the experienced and powerful Roman forces. Boiorix laughed at this soldier's impotence, and instead of withdrawing his soldiers, he instead had the Roman legate executed.

When word of the picket group's decimation and the execution of one of his respected legates reached Gnaeus Mallius Maximus, he looked to his ally across the Rhone, Quintus Servilius Caepio, for backup. However, Caepio refused to move his troops, as this would mean following the orders of the other proconsul. Word of his stubbornness reached the Senate, and they soon sent word to Caepio that he was to merge his forces with Mallius immediately. Not one to balk at orders from the Senate, Caepio led his legion across the Rhone and set up camp, albeit independently of Mallius's camp.

Caepio was not going to take the chance that Mallius would negotiate with the barbarians or somehow rout them. So, he took the initiative and attacked the Cimbri in their own camp. The Roman leader had not foreseen the might of the Cimbrian defense, so very little planning was done when it came to the actual attack of the camp. The battle was over in the blink of an eye, with Caepio's forces being decimated. The Roman leader was able to escape injury and flee back to Mallius's camp. With Cimbrian warriors following close behind, this left Caepio's camp open to being pillaged and ransacked. Not only was his camp left wide open, but the camp he fled to was also left without defenses as well.

The soldiers waiting in the other camp watched as Caepio's camp was taken, and if the option had been there, they would have fled that very moment. But the camp was backed up against the river, which made it impossible for them to cross easily, especially considering the weight of Roman armor. Unable to escape, the soldiers gathered and attempted to stand their ground. Unfortunately, the might of the Germanic warriors and the ill-advised placement of the camp didn't give the Romans any advantage, and it didn't take long for the Roman legion to be laid to waste. The battle was utterly devastating and a great setback for Rome itself.

Not only was the path deeper into Roman territory open, but at the Battle of Arausio, the Romans had also lost more than eighty thousand soldiers. This, coupled with the other defeats around the republic, was beginning to send the people of Rome into a panic. However, instead of moving deeper into Roman territory, the Cimbrian horde opted to move west and test their luck with the tribes of the Iberian Peninsula. This course correction of the horde gave Rome a chance to reorganize as well as to find someone who was experienced enough to fend off the Cimbrian forces upon their inevitable return.

Chapter 6 – The Romans Need an Army

The answer to Rome's problem came in the form of Gaius Marius, a well-respected Roman general who had returned to Rome from a victory in North Africa. Marius was not only a Senate favorite, but his soldiers were also devoted to him. It seemed as if he was the perfect choice to lead the soldiers who would fend off the Cimbrian forces. With the Germanic tribes raiding and pillaging the Iberian Peninsula, Marius began rebuilding the Roman army. Unfortunately for Marius, it proved more difficult than he had thought to recruit and build a new army. There had already been massive numbers of deaths during the initial conflicts with the Cimbri.

With recruits being hard to find, Marius had to take unheard-of actions in tandem with the Roman Senate changing the rules of the Roman recruitment system. At the beginning of his tenure as the head of the Roman forces, only those who owned land or had money were able to enlist as Roman soldiers. With the changes, Marius and the Senate allowed those who were poor or landless to join the army. The idea of earning a set salary and the promise of land incentivized many men to join the legions. Marius also sent messengers to the outlying territories to build his ranks as fast as possible.

Among the many territories outside of Rome that Marius sent word to was Bithynia (which is now north-central Turkey). King Nicomedes III received the request, but with the Roman tax collectors being so prudent with their jobs, there were no men that he could send since most of the able-bodied men had been forced into slavery due to the harsh taxes. This knowledge was shocking to the Senate, and they immediately moved to change the rules, saying that no freeman in any of Rome's territories or allies should be forced into slavery due to tax collection.

The Bithynian king was not the only ruler to find this demand challenging; in fact, the praetor of Sicily, Licinius Nerva, also had the same problem. With the new decree of the Roman Senate coming down, Nerva sent out a proclamation. This proclamation stated that if there were any slaves on the island who felt themselves wrongfully enslaved due to taxes, they should come forward and present evidence to earn their freedom. Many slaves appeared before him to gain their freedom, and after several days of hearings, more than eight hundred men had proven that they deserved liberation from their masters. In response, many of the prominent Romans on the island banded together to coerce the praetor to reverse his decree and return their slaves to them.

With pressure mounting on all sides and with a sizable amount of money from the Roman elite, Nerva decided to stand against the Roman Senate's decree and retract the freedom that he had given the slaves. A new edict was sent out that stated that all slaves who had received liberation were expected to return to their masters and that any slaves who were still waiting for a ruling were dismissed.

The slaves knew the horrors that were waiting for them upon their return, so they chose to find a central location where they could discuss how they could stand up to this betrayal. The slaves took up residence at the Citadel of the Twins in a grove near Palici lake.

Tired of the poor treatment and emboldened by their recent brush with freedom, the slaves discussed many topics, including the rebellion that was brewing. After this meeting, the slaves disbanded, finding shelter in many of the homes across Sicily. The gathering, though, had lit a fire in many of the slaves, including numerous slaves who were owned by a pair of rich Romans in Haliciae. Led by a slave named Varius, thirty of these slaves united together to take their freedom. Varius knew that freedom was not possible as long as their masters were still breathing, so he urged his small gang to kill their masters. The band of slaves snuck into their masters' home in the dead of night, and while their masters laid in bed, they took their lives.

Once the slaves had freed themselves from their owners, they moved onto farms and homes nearby. As they moved from place to place, the small band grew to a force of more than 120 men. Now with a decent force, Varius and his small army established a base of operations near the town of Engyion. There they prepared themselves for the impending Roman attack by fortifying the already sturdy structure. Over the several days that it took to fortify their location, many more slaves found their way to this bastion of hope. There was no way that Licinius Nerva could allow this to continue, so he took eighty men and moved to meet these slaves.

When Nerva and his men reached the slaves' stronghold, it was very obvious that the rebellion would not be easily squashed using force. So, Nerva used his wits and opted to infiltrate the fortress and conquer it from within. He knew there was a brigand roaming the province that had escaped captivity after being sentenced to death. The man known as Titinius would certainly want his record expunged so that he could live a normal life. With this knowledge, Nerva sent word and was able to procure the criminal's services in infiltrating the slave citadel.

Knowing that the slaves would be suspicious of a single man, Titinius gathered together a small body of slaves and appeared before the gates of the fort. He told the guards that he was looking to join them to take his revenge on the Romans who had imprisoned him. These words were the right ones to gain him admittance into the fortress. Once inside, he was greeted by Varius, who welcomed Titinius with open arms. Upon learning of who he was, Varius quickly suggested that he take charge of the army itself as the general. This played right into Nerva's and Titinius's plan. Now with full control over the fortress and the troops within it, Titinius was in place to make his move.

Titinius suggested that the forces make some sort of move on the enemies sitting outside the fortress. Knowing full well that the soldiers of the slave army would not pose a challenge for the Roman soldiers who awaited them, he maneuvered the troops he had been given control over into the waiting hands of Nerva. The Roman soldiers quickly routed the rebels, killing some during the battle but capturing a large majority of them. Like his predecessors before him, Nerva knew he had to send a message to the remaining slaves in Sicily in order to ensure the rebellion was squashed. To do this, he utilized the classic Roman tactic of crucifying his captives.

The slaves who managed to avoid capture opted to take their own lives instead of being crucified. They hurled themselves from the steep rocky crags above the battlefield. Nerva was bolstered by his victory, as he felt that he had single-handedly stopped the slave rebellion in its tracks. Not wanting to incur any more costs, he dismissed the recently conscripted men in his forces, allowing them to return to their homes and their lives.

In reality, though, this was just the first of many uprisings that would go down in history as the Second Servile War. The remaining soldiers returned to their base, where they were greeted with news of yet another slave uprising, this time on the southeastern coast of the island.

Utilizing the lull in work on the estate of Publius Clonius, his slaves, who were inspired by Varius, concocted a plan to achieve their freedom. Using special signals, the slaves were able to make their way into their master's house. They quietly waited for the right moment to slit the prominent Roman's throat.

In hindsight, Nerva's decision to disband his militia was a mistake. He now had to recall them, which allowed the new slave army to build a force that could rival the Roman forces on the island. Hearing of Clonius's slaves' success, slaves from many estates around the area began to flock to the slaves' encampment along the Alba River near Mount Caprianus.

Nerva knew that he needed to move on the slaves as soon as possible, and that meant taking the shortest route, which was by water. So as soon as he was able to muster the appropriate number of men, he packed his forces onto one of his many ships and began sailing south. As he neared the Alba River, Nerva was struck by a sudden thought—the slave army would be able to see them going past if they came the direct route. So, instead of weighing anchor and attacking from the river, he sailed past the encampment and headed toward the city of Heraclea.

When word of Nerva's vessel passing by reached the slaves, they thought that perhaps the Roman praetor was scared, and this incited many more slaves to join the encampment. Within the week it took the Roman forces to make landfall, the slave army's ranks increased to over two thousand men. When Nerva did reach land, the Roman leaders were quick to inform him of the rapidly increasing forces waiting for him. But Nerva still felt that the training and experience of his troops would make up the difference, and he sent Marcus Titinius with six hundred men from the city of Enna to stamp out this new rebellion.

Marcus Titinius marched his well-equipped and somewhat experienced men toward the slave encampment. He was confident that the battle would be quick and decisive. Unfortunately for the

Roman general, the slaves had advantages that he might not have been aware of, such as a strategic position that was easily defendable. Though the slaves were armed with simple weapons like sickles and clubs, they had the passion and drive and were able to withstand the Romans' repetitive charges into their encampment. Eventually, the determination of the slave army won out, and many of the Roman soldiers, feeling that all was lost, dropped their weapons and fled the battlefield. Their weapons now lay on the ground for the slaves to pick up and utilize, not only in this battle but also in the coming ones. The slaves chased after the retreating Romans, and they took their vengeance on as many soldiers as they could.

The resounding defeat of the Roman troops gave courage to many of the remaining slaves to break their shackles as well. Within a week of the slaves' victory, the slave army had amassed around six thousand men and women. With so many now gathered, it became clear that there needed to be some organization and someone at the head of the army. A gathering was called, where these topics were addressed. First and foremost, they needed to have a leader, and after looking within their ranks, the majority felt there was no better man to lead the way than Salvius Tryphon. After all, much like the leader of the previous slave rebellion, Salvius was one of the slaves who began this uprising, and he had played a key part in the victory they had just experienced. On top of that, much like Eunus, the great leader of the slave uprising who had become King Antiochus of Sicily, Salvius had once been a reputed seer. And Salvius was a king himself.

Salvius knew that though the numbers had swollen in their ranks, they would be no match if Rome decided to send more legions to crush the rebellion. He was also fully aware that there were still pockets of the island where slaves had yet to be freed. With this in mind, he began organizing his troops by separating them into three squadrons and appointing a general for each. For the women and children, he assigned them menial tasks, like cooking and tending to wounds. Once Salvius had done this, he made each general march in a specific direction. These generals were free to recruit as many of the slaves as they could. After they had made their circle through their designated area, each of the generals was to return to the same place to join together into one giant army.

After weeks of marching, the generals converged at the meeting point, bringing the men and supplies they were able to procure on their marches. King Salvius now stood at the head of somewhere around twenty thousand soldiers. Along with this, the generals brought plenty of horses, cattle, and sheep in order to supply their newly formed army with everything they needed to defeat the Roman praetor still in charge of the island.

But there was a problem: the men who stood before him were raw and undertrained. So, before Salvius could begin his march on any of the well-fortified cities, he had to train his troops. Now in command of more than two thousand horses, the first order of business was to begin training a calvary. Salvius then began training the infantrymen, arming them with the weapons that had been claimed during the last battle. The first city on Salvius's itinerary was the mighty fortress of Morgantina, as he knew this would be a major blow to the Roman forces governing Sicily.

While Salvius was whipping his troops into shape, Roman praetor Nerva began building his forces as well. He was well aware that Rome's troubles with the rebel slaves were not over by a long shot. By pulling together the remaining soldiers from the last encounter and merging them with forces recruited from the island itself, as well as soldiers sent from the mainland, he was able to amass a legion of ten thousand men. He marched his men night and day in the hopes that he could reach the mighty citadel before the rebels could. However, he was unable to meet his goals, as Salvius and his men had already begun besieging the citadel.

Salvius and his troops solely paid attention to bringing down the citadel, which meant they left their encampment with very little supervision. The Roman general seized the opportunity and surprised the rebel encampment. Making quick work of the camp, he took the supplies that he needed and continued his march to break the siege of Morgantina. Salvius's troops, who had finally found a secure spot to attack the citadel, received word of the attack on their encampment. In fear for those they had left behind, the slave forces rushed back to charge headlong into the waiting Roman legion.

Even though the Roman general had expected that his enemies would turn on him, he was not prepared for their discipline and strength. He had also not accounted for the fact that some of his men were slaves. Salvius realized this, and he stopped and declared that any slave who wanted to be free should throw down their weapons and join him. Not wanting to live their lives being ruled by others, some of the soldiers within the ranks of the Roman troops began throwing their weapons to the ground. Some broke away and joined the slave king, while others simply fled the battlefield altogether.

Not only did this cause panic within the Roman troops, but it also allowed Salvius to reclaim the supplies and arms that the Romans had procured from the camp they had just raided. As the Roman legions began to flee in fear, Salvius and his troops pursued them. In the end, they were able to capture four thousand Roman soldiers. Once the battle was done, King Salvius and his slave army were able to build their armor and equipment to brand-new levels.

With this distraction taken care of, Salvius's troops returned their attention to the fortress of Morgantina. However, during this time, the Roman general in charge of the citadel was able to fortify his position by offering freedom to the slaves within if they sided with him as opposed to the slave king knocking at their door. The slaves, who were more than likely afraid of the unknown, chose to side with the Roman general. The slaves within the fortress fought with fervor, expecting their leaders to stand behind their words when the battle concluded. Ultimately, the people of Morgantina were able to make King Salvius and his forces pull back from the siege.

With the siege broken, the slaves turned to their masters, waiting for their liberation, but it quickly became evident that they had never intended to live up to their word. The slaves within the citadel then turned and opted to switch sides, taking King Salvius up on his previous offer. By adding these slaves to his ever-expanding forces, Salvius had enough power to take the citadel, sending a strong message to Rome. The slaves of Sicily would not give up easily.

Chapter 7 – The Second Servile War

Salvius's slave rebellion was not the only one that was taking place at this time. On the western coast of the island, another slave was taking inspiration from the recent successes. Athenion was a Cilician (an ancient country that is now located in southeast Turkey) who had elevated himself above the other slaves of his two very rich owners. He was smart, and due to his diligence, he had been given control of two hundred of his Roman masters' herdsmen. Athenion had also begun to build a reputation amongst his men as a leader. Thus, when it came time to stand up and overthrow their masters, the two hundred men were more than willing to stand behind Athenion. His family and the rest of the slaves of the estate, though, were forced to toil away in the slave pits. Athenion knew that after his plan had been executed, he would first unleash the slaves there in hopes their gratitude would lead them to join his cause.

Finally, after hearing of the slave revolt of Salvius and his men, Athenion knew it was time. He sent word to his two hundred men, and without question, they rushed on their masters, killing them. The plan went accordingly, and soon those men and Athenion set upon the slave pits, releasing all the men, women, and children kept there from their shackles. Many of the released slaves decide to stay and seek recruitment in Athenion's army. Within just a few days, that two hundred men grew into thousands, and Athenion began to feel the effects of holding all the power. Athenion gradually went from being the slaves' benevolent liberator and leader to a prophet and messiah. It was all part of his plan, as he knew it would be the only way to control his fellow slaves.

Because of his connection with powers the slaves didn't understand and also because he had freed them, the slaves crowned him king. With this new power added to his already illustrious reputation, Athenion took note of where there were faults in the plans of the previous slave rebellion leaders. He came to the conclusion that their problem was that they took anyone into their army. So, instead of following in their footsteps, King Athenion took special care when evaluating those who came before him. He would take only the bravest, most obedient, and strongest into his ranks. The rejected slaves were sent back to continue cultivating the land and breeding livestock. Athenion knew that famine could be a greater death sentence than the masses of legions being sent to the island.

Now with an army of able-bodied men and a supply train that would keep his men fed well, Athenion knew he needed to make his position more secure. Athenion began to talk of his connections with the gods. He began stargazing more and prophesized that he was foretold to take control over all of Sicily. He would relay to his people that though there would be great battles, his people could rely on him to protect the land and crops since they all would belong to him in the end. These prophecies spread across the region and brought more and more recruits into his army. In time, Athenion oversaw ten thousand men, and he knew he needed a big victory to prove his worth. So, he set his sights on the well-fortified city of Lilybaeum (modern-day Marsala).

The slave army set up camp outside the walls of the mighty city and readied itself for what could potentially be a lengthy siege. For weeks, Athenion and his forces laid siege to the city, and even with their determination and the ruler's prophecies, they gained no headway on cracking the city's defenses. Realizing all was lost, Athenion had to come up with a way to back out of the siege and not ruin his reputation with his people. The slave king looked to the stars and the gods for the right answer. After a long night of stargazing, Athenion stood before his troops and imparted the words he had received from the gods. It seems the gods did not look favorably on the siege and warned that if the siege continued, there would be little hope for a victory. In fact, ultimate disaster would befall the army if they continued. Once these words had been relayed, Athenion's forces were more than ready to break camp and move on to their next conquest.

But while the slave army had been laying siege to the city, its Roman leaders found a way to send word to their allies for reinforcements. The ally that answered the call was King Bocchus I of Mauritania (modern-day Algeria and northern Morocco), but it took his small fleet a while to reach the island. The fleet arrived in the city's harbor under cover of night, and its commander, Gomon, decided to attack immediately. Athenion's troops had already broken the siege and were about to slink away in the night when Gomon and his troops attacked. Surprised, Athenion and his troops retreated as fast as possible. Unfortunately for them, the Mauritanian sailors were fast and well trained. The attacking forces were able to take out a good number of Athenion's troops and return to Lilybaeum victorious.

Although the Mauritanians were victorious, their victory served to cement Athenion's ability to be a conduit of the gods, which helped him continue his reign. Along with that, this defeat also changed Athenion's focus when it came to his plan of attack. He now understood that the fortress-like Lilybaeum would fall all on its own if the slaves within the walls began to believe there was some hope for liberation from their harsh Roman masters. Instead, Athenion began looking at taking smaller cities and country estates. This would give him control over the island's resources, which he could then keep from reaching the citadels. It would be simple to watch them fall one by one without expending his forces or resources.

But it wasn't only the Romans that the newly crowned king had to deal with. Without the strict hand of the Roman praetor overseeing the conditions on the island, the poor freemen were also up in arms. Since they had to feed their families, many of these men resorted to any means necessary to obtain food or money, including robbery and murder. These men didn't care what side someone was on; they just wanted to ensure their ends were met. This resulted in a Sicily filled with pockets of lawlessness. This was challenging, but it in no way deterred either Salvius or Athenion in their efforts. In fact, this served to bolster both armies, as many of these unhappy freemen found their way into the slave army's ranks. These extra troops helped Athenion defeat several Roman forces.

While all of this was going on, Salvius was still making moves to cement his newly formed kingdom. After his siege of Morgantina, he made plans to create a capital. For this, he decided that the best location for his palace would be Triocala (modern-day Caltabellotta). But he knew that he would need assistance. Salvius had heard of Athenion's uprising in the south, so he sent word for the other slave leader to make his way north to him. Though he had heard of Athenion's crowning as king, Salvius still saw himself as the only true king of Sicily, which would, of course, eventually cause problems between the two down the road. But for now, the two alphas were open to working together. So, Athenion sent some of his troops out into the countryside and ordered them to continue recruitment. He then took three thousand men and marched north.

The two leaders met at Triocala. Salvius had chosen this place for its lush vineyard, access to water, and the easy defensive position it would afford his new palace. Once the capital was built and fortified, King Salvius began to build his government, choosing to use the method of the Romans. These councilmen and lictors (men chosen to act as magistrates and councilors) would often stroll the streets in their purple clothing, jewels, and weapons, making sure the city maintained its respectable reputation. Salvius then immediately ordered his troops and Athenion's to begin construction on his palace. This palace was designed with high walls, a moat, and a lavish estate.

After a while, though, Salvius began to be suspicious of Athenion and his ulterior motives. Feeling that it was only a matter of time before Athenion would challenge him for the throne, Salvius had the southern slave leader arrested and imprisoned for treason.

In 103 BCE, the king received some distressing news: the Roman Senate had found a new candidate in their mission to put an end to the slave rebellion on Sicily. Lucius Licinius Lucullus had just raised his status with his most recent triumph over a slave rebellion in Campania (a region in southwestern Italy). The previous year (104 BCE), Lucullus had been appointed to a praetorship, and in a short amount of time, he found himself on the hunt for a fugitive knight who had instigated a slave revolt. Titus Minucius Vettius was an Eques (a Roman knight) in Capua, a city within the Campania region, who had run into some troubles after falling in love with a slave girl. Unable to fulfill his part of a deal he had entered into with several creditors, Vettius found the answer to his problem in murder. Knowing that he wanted to have clear access to the slave girl, he captured and killed both the creditors, as well as his beloved's master. Vettius then continued his rebellion against the system by releasing and arming the slaves.

To make his claim as the leader of the revolution, the lovestruck knight also proclaimed himself the new king of Campania. This proclamation meant he could make decrees, like freeing the slaves in the region. Many slaves across Campania heard his words and escaped from their masters to join him in Capua. With an army of over six hundred men, Vettius began raiding the region and absorbing any slaves who were freed by the raids. Those that chose not to break their shackles found themselves experiencing the same fate as their Roman masters—death.

News of this uprising finally reached Rome, and the Senate acted quickly to appoint someone to take care of the problem. They chose the new praetor Lucius Licinius Lucullus, and backed by 4,400 men, he began his march to Capua. Vettius had heard that Lucullus was marching on him, so he moved his men to the top of a hill that he felt would give them somewhat of a strategic advantage. Once there, he and his men worked tirelessly to fortify the hill. It wasn't long before the Roman leader and his army approached the location, and the two forces immediately clashed. Lucullus's first attempt was easily repelled simply because of Vettius's smart placement of his troops.

It was clear to Lucullus that he was dealing with an accomplished strategist, so he decided that he would have to use a different tactic. Lucullus sent a message via a spy to Vettius's general, Apollonius, offering him safety and freedom if he were to help the Roman praetor end the rebellion. Apollonius knew that the Roman forces would eventually win out, and he also knew what they would do to the rebels afterward. So, he chose to save his own life and betray Vettius. This division of the slave forces allowed the Roman legion to come out on top.

To save himself, Vettius took his own life after he realized that there was no hope for victory. Lucullus kept his word to Apollonius and returned victorious to Rome. This made Lucullus the perfect candidate to take on the slave rebellion in Sicily. He was outfitted with over sixteen thousand men for this new campaign in Sicily, and he was intent on being victorious.

Accompanied by the respected Roman general Cleptius, Lucullus marched his troops into Sicily, heading toward the capital city of Triocala. Salvius was feeling the noose tighten, so he sent someone to bring Athenion to him from the prison he had been rotting in for some time. The king offered Athenion his freedom and appointed him a general once again. Salvius immediately began picking his brain when it came to the proper tactics they needed to use to ensure victory against the Roman invaders. Salvius felt it would be best to stay in the fortified walls of Triocala, but Athenion said that would be a mistake. Instead, he advised that he and the king's men head out and meet the Roman forces on an open battlefield. Staying in the walls of the capital would open them up to a siege that they may not be able to withstand.

The king agreed, and Athenion rode out with more than forty thousand troops to meet the Roman forces on the open plain of Scirthaea. Athenion set up his camp about twelve miles from Lucullus and began to prepare for battle. Though Athenion had the advantage in numbers, his troops were not as disciplined or trained as their Roman counterparts, so Lucullus felt that he would win in the end.

The two armies spent days executing battles that were very light. Each side quickly felt the fervor of conflict, and growing tired of the light skirmishes, they became locked in all-out combat. During the battle, Athenion felt the rush of battle and mounted his horse, charging headlong into the battle while being backed by several hundred of his cavalrymen. Roman soldier after Roman soldier fell to Athenion's cavalry, and it looked like the slave army was on its way to victory. Then a blow was delivered that would change the course of the battle in favor of the Romans.

As Athenion trampled through the Roman forces, he was suddenly struck down from his horse. A Roman soldier had been able to deal severe wounds to the mighty general's legs. After he had fallen from his horse, he was struck one more time. He just lay there, unable to fight. Seeing this, his soldiers began to panic, and this caught the eye of the Roman soldiers, who were made aware that the slave army's leader had fallen. They then rallied and charged into the fighting with more passion than before. This, of course, exacerbated the panic of the slave army, and it wasn't long before many of them were flying back to the safety of Triocala, watching as the Roman legions began mercilessly killing many of their fellow soldiers.

Athenion was still alive, but he chose to feign death and keep himself hidden until the Roman soldiers had left the battlefield. Under cover of night, Athenion raised himself from the piles of corpses around him and found his way back into the citadel.

Salvius and Athenion convened together to discuss the previous battle, and though they had lost, they felt they had dealt a devastating blow to Lucullus's army. Knowing this, they began to work on the fortifications of Triocala because they knew Lucullus would be on their doorstep soon.

Due to the devastating blow dealt by the slave army, it took Lucullus more than a week to find his way to the slave king's citadel. Athenion stood at the head of his army once again, and he agreed with Salvius that they should prepare for anything, including a long siege. But the Roman praetor and his general wanted to end this rebellion as quickly as possible, so instead of laying siege to the city, they chose to rush headlong into battle. On the wide-open field in front of the city, the Roman legion led the first attack against the rebel army. The battle was bloody, but unlike Scirthaea, the victory went to Athenion's forces. Lucullus's camp was decimated, and they were routed from it as well.

This first devastating loss was to be the first in a long line of attempts by the Roman praetor to take the city. Eventually, Lucullus came to terms with the fact that his soldiers were not going to be able to take the city, and instead, they hunkered down for an extended siege. The siege lasted throughout the year. By then, the Senate finally realized that Lucullus would not be able to defeat the slave rebellion, even though he had succeeded in taking Salvius's life during one of the incessant assaults. The Senate decided it was time for a new leader and ordered Lucullus back to Rome.

Lucullus was devastated by this decision and felt betrayed by his superiors. His disappointment turned into anger upon hearing of the arrival of his replacement. To make his voice heard, the Roman praetor disbanded his horses and had his men destroy any supplies they had left, as well as the siege equipment. Without these, he knew that his replacement, Gaius Servilius, would be less successful than he was.

However, this disastrous decision led to a trial upon his return home to Rome in 102 BCE. Lucullus was charged with abusing his command, and he was found guilty. Lucullus was banished from Rome for the remainder of his life.

With the command of the Roman army now firmly in the hands of Gaius Servilius, he marched his army from Messana to meet Athenion's forces, who had been crowned king after Salvius's death. Servilius moved his troops southwest of Messana, marching headlong toward conflict with Athenion and his troops. Eventually, the two mighty forces clashed, and in their first battle, thanks to the sabotage of Lucullus, the new praetor was at a disadvantage.

After several devastating skirmishes, the slave king knew he had superiority over the Roman legions, and he began to take advantage of his position. Athenion would march throughout the island, laying waste to the country and decimating towns and cities. Eventually, he turned his focus on Messana. He marched on the city and launched a night attack, where he killed many and plundered the city for supplies. The powerful slave king then decided it was time for him to set up his own capital. Athenion marched west, setting up his citadel in Macella, an ancient walled city. He began to fortify the city and build up supplies for his army, knowing that more Roman soldiers would come.

Many things occurred on the Roman side of the conflict during all of this. First and foremost, like Lucullus before him, Servilius found himself unable to stop the slave rebellion and eventually was called back to Rome to meet the same fate as his predecessor. In 101 BCE, another consul was charged with stopping the rebellion and defeating the slave army in Sicily; that man was Manius Aquillius.

Outfitted with several well-trained and experienced cohorts from the frontlines of Gaul that had been sent by Gaius Marius, Aquillius landed on the island, ready to do the impossible. His legion was constructed of veteran soldiers, and thanks to the ravages committed against the people of Sicily, many people joined the Roman ranks. This also included the remaining armies of both of the previous praetors.

As the newly appointed Roman general moved toward the fortified city of Macella, he took the time to train those recruited into his ranks who hadn't had the proper training. By doing this, he had a force that far surpassed Athenion's, as well as any of the previous Roman generals who tried to quell this revolt.

Athenion did not want to repeat the mistakes of any of his predecessors, so he opted to march out to meet the new Roman general on the battlefield. The battle raged on, and eventually, Athenion and Aquillius found themselves in one-on-one combat. The two fought valiantly, but Aquillius was able to maneuver so that he delivered a mortal blow. Athenion collapsed to the ground, and upon seeing this, his troops fell back, with many of them fleeing into the mountains around the battlefield. The Roman general gave chase to the retreating slave army.

With very few men left in the slave army, a new leader stepped up to lead. Satyrus stood in front of the now devastated slave army and spoke to them about their bravery and continuing the fight that Salvius and Athenion had believed so strongly in.

At first, the Roman general decided to use force to exterminate the slave rebellion, but he eventually began utilizing their submission instead. Though he had taken more than twenty thousand prisoners, the rebellion was not over until the leaders were gone and the army was decimated to the point of no return. Though some of the forces made their way into the mountains and continued to be thorns in the sides of the Romans for the next two years, the majority of the slave army was taken prisoner and sent to Rome to fight in the arena against wild beasts. This, of course, included Satyrus, who watched as his fellow freedom fighters were forced to die in the pits against wild beasts. Supposedly, instead of battling the beasts, the slaves killed each other in protest. If this is true, Satyrus certainly would have opted to take his own life instead of being forced to amuse the Romans.

Aquillius returned to Rome victorious, having put an end to the four-year-long war that Rome had fought to regain control of Sicily. Though the war was over and Aquillius was victorious, the same fate would befall him as the previous two praetors. He was accused of mismanaging his forces, but unlike the other praetors, he was acquitted. However, he still had a tragic ending to his story. In 89 BCE, he was engaged in a military campaign against Mithridates VI of Pontus and was captured. According to some ancient scholars, a year later, Mithridates would execute him by pouring molten gold down his throat.

Chapter 8 – Gladiators and Their Lives

During the 1st and 2nd centuries BCE, Rome expanded greatly and had taken part in many wars. Because of this, the growing republic was inundated with hundreds of thousands of slaves from all over the world. These slaves did everything from being household servants to working in the fields, particularly in southern Italy and on the island of Sicily. Slaves led an agonizing life, and due to Roman apathy, they were not even considered people. These men, women, and children were considered property by many estate owners and thus were treated poorly. Of course, even amongst the slaves, there were different tiers, but they all existed in the same category in the eyes of the average Roman citizen.

The mass number of slaves that were brought into the Roman Republic at that time is what brought about the First and Second Servile Wars. These wars were nothing more than civil disturbances to the Roman leadership. They took years and manpower to end, but they were never a serious threat to the republic itself. After all, these disruptions had happened on the island of Sicily, not on the mainland, where the effects and consequences of the conflicts could be felt by the Roman elite. But all that was soon to change when the ramifications of the Romans' treatment of the slaves would finally be felt on the mainland. This time, the slave revolt would be led by warrior slaves, otherwise known as gladiators. To understand the actions of these slaves who would shake the foundations of the Roman Republic, one first needs to understand the life and history of the gladiator.

In the early part of the Roman Republic's growth, armed combat outside of a conflict would not be seen unless soldiers were being trained or there was some event like a funeral. Oftentimes at these funerals, one could watch chariot races, competitions of athletic prowess, and theatrical reenactments of great deeds from the deceased's past. These funerals were major affairs and often were even open to the public. At the early beginning of these grand funerals, the games would be set up close to the tomb of the deceased individual they were looking to commemorate. These would be lavish affairs organized by what was known as a munerator. Eventually, as the popularity of these traditions grew, they became more lavish and required more arrangements. These then included a second individual known as an editor, who acted as the munerator or was an assistant of said individual.

As the years went on, these two titles became synonymous with each other. In addition, these events began to be more widespread, even finding their way into private citizens' homes. Citizens were even able to own their own gladiators as long as they had permission from the emperor. Because of this, the position of editor was raised to a state title.

This tradition of funerals is what gave birth to the larger-scale reenactments that were prominent in the colosseums of the Roman Republic and Roman Empire. And as the legislative powers began to be more and more intertwined with this tradition, it became a note of pride to be able to foot the costs of these games. For the smaller towns, this was done by the quaestors (an official charged with handling the treasury in the Roman Republic). They took a large portion of their own salary and donated it to the small towns or communities they oversaw. When it came to larger-scale events, these were often backed by people in higher positions, including even the emperor himself after the republic fell.

The first gladiator match has been dated to the 3rd century BCE, but gladiator fights didn't hit their peak until the 1st century BCE. With an ever-expanding republic and later empire, more and more soldiers were taken prisoner, making it much easier to keep the ranks of the gladiators consistently replenished.

In fact, many of the gladiator categories took on the name of these enemy prisoners. Among these include the Thracian, the Gallus (named after the Gauls), and the Samnite. Each of these categories had a specific look and specialty that would make them stand out in the gladiator matches. The Samnite was a gladiator that came out into the arena in full armor; this category eventually became known as the secutor. This form of gladiator wasn't the only one that got a new name as time went by. For instance, the Gallus was rechristened the murmillo.

The games would progress in many different ways; for example, some of the matches had pairings. At the beginning of these labor-intensive spectacles, one would watch gladiators fighting gladiators who had the same fighting style. But as time went on, people wanted to see more novel fights. Thus, it would not be odd to find a retiarius fighting the fully armored secutor. A retiarius would be lightly armored and use a net to ensnare his opponents and a trident to stab them.

Because of the ever-growing popularity of the gladiators themselves, as well as the games, the trade market for slaves boomed. Many of these slaves would find their way not only to the amphitheaters but also to the mines. However, the best of these warrior slaves were naturally sent to Rome, where they spent their life (however short it may be) training as gladiators and working to gain their honor back.

Of course, enslaving enemy warriors was not the only way the Romans maintained the ranks of the gladiator schools. There were also those known as the damnati, people who had committed crimes and been sentenced to fight in the games. Along with these individuals, there were also people who volunteered to be part of the games (known as the auctorati). Sometimes, becoming an auctorati was the best option available for those of the lower classes or individuals who were noncitizens. By signing up for a gladiator school, these individuals not only learned a trade but were also given room and board. Along with this, there was the option of gaining fame and fortune, which would allow them to pull themselves out of poverty.

The iconic image of a gladiator is of a well-muscled man adorned with armor fighting in an arena surrounded by cheering crowds. But men were not the only ones to fight in the arena. In fact, many women found fame in the gladiatorial battles. They didn't become more popular until the Roman Empire, but their popularity lasted all the way to 200 CE. Emperor Septimius Severus decided that it was inappropriate for women to fight and banned the use of female gladiators (also known as gladiatrix). There were also even emperors, such as Commodus, who took the opportunity to stand in the arena and show their prowess on the battlefield.

As the gladiators' popularity grew during the Roman Empire, gladiatorial fights became a way for the emperor to show his people that he cared about them. At these events, he not only would generously host these fights to entertain his people, but he would also show himself, giving him better visibility. The spectacles became so ingrained in the Roman people's lives that in 70 CE, it became evident to Emperor Vespasian that there needed to be a larger arena so more of his citizens could take in the games.

This thought became the ember that would build one of the greatest amphitheaters ever seen in the world: the Colosseum of Rome. The Colosseum took ten years to build and was christened by a one-hundred-day celebration that was offered to the Roman people by Emperor Titus, who completed construction on the amphitheater.

Even before the mighty Colosseum was built, there were many gladiators spread throughout the country who were learning their skills at schools. Soon, many gladiator schools (known then as ludi) across the republic were opened. In these schools, criminals and prisoners that had been taken during conquests were taught the skills needed for competition in the amphitheaters across the country.

Before their training commenced, there were a few steps that had to be taken care of to ensure that the gladiators knew their duty and their place. These men would swear an oath, dedicating their lives to their training and their masters. For those who had been condemned, they would be marked with either a tattoo or branding so that wherever they went, they knew their crimes and their punishment. At these schools, men were trained on the sandy floors of arenas to not only handle one-on-one combat but also fights against wild animals. Each of the gladiators would be trained in a specific category depending on their method of fighting. For those who were captured in battle, they were often allowed to utilize the weapons they were most familiar with, but for those who had no skills, the master would have to evaluate them. Once they had been evaluated, they were placed in a category and trained to fight in that style.

The novice gladiators would train under experienced gladiators within the school, and through hard work and dedication, they would make their way up the ladder in an attempt to reach the highest rank: primus palus. Regardless of their ultimate rank, each of these gladiators would endure harsh training, gradually becoming mighty specimens that would entertain the masses. During training sessions, they never used lethal weapons. It almost seems like they were rehearsing for a play, a play in which men might die. It was best to have no emotion if such a thing were to happen, as it would help to prove their strength.

To some, this may seem like a glorious way to live and die, but the daily life of these gladiators was very different than the spectacle of the arena. These beloved celebrities were still nothing more than slaves and tended to be locked away at night in cells that were little better than a common jail. These cells were crafted in barrack-like buildings around a training area. Each barrack was dedicated to a certain division of gladiators. The masters of the schools were very careful to ensure that gladiators who may become opponents were kept separate from each other in order to reduce the risk of any potential issues arising both in and out of the arena.

These men were woken at the first sign of light every morning, and their day began with a hearty meal. Even though they were slaves, gladiators were allowed better nourishment and lived in more hygienic conditions than your typical slave or even average Roman citizen. After all, their performance was what made their masters money, so an undernourished and sickly gladiator would be counterproductive. Gladiators also had to endure trials and tribulations that made their life challenging and maddening. These mighty warriors were unable to speak except during mealtimes, and when they were not training, they were often kept shackled. When it came to hygiene, their owners wanted to eliminate the chance of disease, so gladiators were allowed to take hot and cold baths. They were also fed three times a day to ensure their health remained at optimal levels. These meals typically were heavier in vegetables and grains than meat, though they were fed fish and meat.

As mentioned above, the health of the gladiators was very important to their masters, as they were a big investment. This meant that they needed to keep their property healthy, and that included things like regular massages and access to physicians of the highest standard.

Once a gladiator had been fully trained, they, along with their families, were then sold to the highest bidder and continued their existence, fighting for whatever Roman noble had paid for them.

No matter what type of gladiator one was or how one found their way into the school, the danger and excitement that these spectacles created gave the Roman people something to think about other than their difficult everyday lives. That is why during the 1st century BCE, most people, no matter their status, spent their downtime attending gladiatorial games, which quickly became the most popular form of entertainment.

But the spectacle was so much more than just the matches in the arena. There was order and systems put in place to ensure that the spectators got what they came for.

Like the spectator sports of today, the preparations for these games started with advertising. For the layperson, this meant sending out word of who was putting on the event, as well as where, when, and the number of gladiators that were going to be present. These also often contained things like notices of executions and the music and other events that would be going on during the game. Music was a big part of the gladiatorial games; it would even be played during the interludes to keep spectators amused and calm.

Oftentimes outside of the venue, there would be people selling food, drinks, and other novelties. For those spectators who were inclined to bet on the gladiatorial outcomes, they were issued different programs that talked about the pairings, as well as the records of each gladiator.

The night before the events, the gladiators themselves were thrown a great feast and given time to take care of their personal affairs. It seemed that this was intended to be the last meal in case they didn't make it out of the gladiatorial games the next day.

Like the systems in place before the game, the actual gladiatorial events had more pomp and circumstance than one might think. Depending on the era, this might include a procession of important magistrates and men in high positions. After this came trumpeters and idols of the gods, as well as a scribe and other individuals meant to honor the events. At the back of that procession marched the gladiators that were set to fight that day.

Typically, the gladiatorial events would begin with matches that involved wild beasts captured in far-off lands. This would be followed by executions and occasionally warm-up matches for the gladiators. Then the gladiators would come out to entertain the crowd. The spectators were more enthralled when the gladiators were evenly matched. Depending on the type of gladiator competing, these matches often took anywhere from ten to twenty minutes at a time. Those gladiators who fell short of courage and hesitated to enter the arena would find themselves in a world of pain, as the punishment for this was being whipped or prodded with hot irons.

These warrior slaves had rules they had to follow, and because of this, referees were present to ensure that they were doing just that. A match was only won when one gladiator submitted or was killed. For those who wanted to submit, they simply would raise a finger in the air to the referee. This request was weighed for its entertainment value. For the most part, though, the wish to submit was granted. However, this might bring dishonor upon the gladiator, as the more respectable end would be death.

If a gladiator was deemed to have died a good death, they were ceremonially removed from the arena on a couch and taken to the morgue. These respected gladiators would then have the armor removed to ensure they were actually dead, and they may have had their throats cut as well. The bodies of those deemed to have died a disrespectful death were removed and often thrown into a river or a dump, where they would be left unburied for wild animals to desecrate.

The life of a gladiator was not a glamorous one, nor was it one that lent itself to a long life. Gladiators usually only lived to see their mid-twenties, and it is thought that as many as 400,000 lost their lives in the arena. So, it is easy to see why men who had fallen into this situation would find it unbearable and eventually rise up to take their lives back.

Chapter 9 – The Gladiators Who Would Shake Rome

Much like other slaves, many men within these schools dreamed of freedom and being able to live their life on their own terms. This passion and desire led the gladiators of the Capua school to rise up and take their freedom back. In 73 BCE, while the mighty Colosseum was still being built, one of the gladiator schools in Capua (which was over one hundred miles southeast of Rome) encountered trouble. This school was run by Lentulus Batiatus (also known as Gnaeus Cornelius Lentulus Vatia). Lentulus's school took in predominantly Gallic and Thracian slaves to train as gladiators. However, he was a cruel master. He kept his gladiators confined almost at all times and gave them the bare necessities. It took weeks and cunning for the two hundred gladiators to plan an escape that would ensure their freedom. However, somehow, their master found out about this plan and began to act accordingly.

Upon realizing that their plan had been discovered, more than seventy of those gladiators, including a Thracian man named Spartacus who was to become the icon of this revolt, took it upon themselves to act quickly. Grabbing knives and spits from the kitchen, the gladiators rushed through the school and found their way out. Once free of the walls of the school, the gladiators knew they had to find a way to slow down the mob that would inevitably come after them. This meant they needed to arm themselves better, so they found a handful of wagons that just so happened to be carrying weapons to gladiators in another city.

Taking advantage of their good luck, these men seized the wagons and quickly got out of the city, moving to a more strategic location where they could defend themselves. The escaped men fought off the small force that was sent after them and then found their way into the countryside. As the well-trained slaves worked their way into the mountains surrounding the area, they found it necessary to plunder estates so that they could clothe and feed themselves. Along the way, their small band grew, as they took in slaves from these estates and armed them as well. The escaped slaves eventually made their way into the mountains and set up camp on the slopes of Mount Vesuvius.

Now free and in a position that they felt was easily defendable, the next step was to establish some kind of leadership. For this, the escaped slaves turned to the men who had been the masterminds behind the escape plan: Crixus, Oenomaus, and, of course, the Thracian instigator Spartacus. These men would not only lead the slaves over the next two years but would also grow this small band of slaves into a mighty army of more than 120,000 men. These forces would defeat Roman leader after Roman leader and leave history with unforgettable scenes of horror. The impact of this slave uprising would be felt for centuries, and it would be the catalyst that helped transform the Roman Republic into the mighty Roman Empire.

The Thracian Spartacus was the first leader the slaves appointed. There are many interpretations of who this gladiator was and from where he came. Most scholars believe he originated from one of the nomadic Thracian tribes (most likely the Maedi tribe). The Thracian lands had been ruled over by many empires, and they spanned a good portion of what is now southeastern Europe (countries like Bulgaria, Greece, and even a portion of northwest Turkey all resided within the borders of Thrace). The warriors of this proud race were prized in war and rode alongside many of the great conquerors of the time like Alexander the Great (356 BCE-323 BCE). After the Third Macedonian War, which ended in 168 BCE, the region was swallowed up by the expanding Roman Republic. But it wasn't until 46 CE that it actually became a Roman province.

It may have been during one of the many uprisings in the Thracian region that Spartacus found himself in the Roman military. (Though how he arrived there depends on the historian; some state that he signed up voluntarily, while others think he became a mercenary who eventually found his way into the legions.) Most agree that at some point, he wound up becoming a prisoner, and because of his prowess and physique, he eventually was sold to a man who would later train him to be a gladiator.

The other two leaders appointed by the slave army were both from the Roman territory of Gaul. Crixus, who eventually became Spartacus's right-hand man, and Oenomaus had both been taken during one of the many skirmishes between the native tribes of the area and Rome as it began to expand. Gaul was part of the western European front, and though many different tribes called it home, the region was primarily settled by the Celtic and the Aquitani tribes. (Gaul would have been located in modern-day France, Belgium, Switzerland, Luxembourg, and even parts of northern Italy, the Netherlands, and Germany.) By the middle of the 2nd century BCE, Rome had conquered a good portion of the region; however, it would not be completely conquered until Julius Caesar arrived on the scene in the 1st century BCE.

Crixus was Gallic, and he most likely fell into the hands of the Roman legions during one of the many battles that took place in Gaul. Crixus had a warrior's physique and experience in warfare, so he found himself being sold into servitude as a gladiator.

The last of the triumvirate to be elected as the leader of the rebellion was Oenomaus. Truthfully, little is known about this gladiator except for the fact that he hailed from Gaul. Like the other two men, most historians believe that this warrior was taken at a young age and sold into slavery, where he eventually found his way into the gladiator school in Capua.

With the task of naming their leaders completed, Spartacus and his forces settled into their camp on Mount Vesuvius. Their camp had a narrow entryway, and there was only one way in. The fortified area was also surrounded by steep crevices on all three sides. From here, the slaves would continue plundering the cities and towns nearby.

Eventually, word of the rebellion found its way to the capital, and soon one of the local praetors, Gaius Claudius Glaber, along with three thousand Roman militiamen, marched on the rebel encampment. Glaber came from a plebeian family and had worked his way up, being elected a praetor in 73 BCE. This uprising would be his first test of prowess, and he intended on making the most of it. Though his militia may have been large, they had yet to see battle and had little to no training. This is because the militia was typically only used for riots or to break up fights.

Glaber knew that his troops were ill-equipped to fight any type of ground battle, so he set up camp at the only entrance up the mountain and laid siege to Spartacus and his men. The Roman praetor and his men would wait patiently to hopefully force the slaves to surrender via starvation. Spartacus's forces were just as green as the troops led by Glaber, but they had something the Roman forces didn't—resourcefulness. Although the rebellious slaves were surrounded on all sides by sheer cliff faces, these cliff faces were covered with long vines that could easily be cut and fashioned into ropes and ladders. Spartacus ordered the men to begin cutting them down and twisting them into ladders that could hold their weight. These ladders would have to be long enough to be able to reach the bottom easily.

The Roman forces were, of course, unaware of the ingenuity of these slaves, so they were unprepared for the attack. Spartacus and his men waited until the sun had gone down. Utilizing their cleverly crafted ladders, they shimmied down and moved around the edge of Vesuvius until they had found themselves behind the Roman camp. As the rebel slaves worked their way around to the camp, they found themselves joined by herdsmen and shepherds from the surrounding area. They quickly dispatched what few militiamen were left to guard the parameters of the camp and rushed on the remaining portion of the camp, easily taking care of the militiamen, who were caught off-guard. Glaber and his militia had been defeated by Spartacus and his men, but the Third Servile War was far from over.

Chapter 10 – The Third Servile War

Rome was irritated, but the government was unwilling to look at this uprising as another war, although that attitude would soon change. The Senate was devastated at the loss of Glaber and quickly sent another praetor to bring the rebel gladiators down. The senators decided that Publius Varinius was the man for the job. Varinius chose to send two armies under separate lieutenants to meet the rebels. These forces were led by lieutenants Lucius Furius and Lucius Cossinius, and each rode forward at the head of two thousand men (it is not known whether these men were Roman legions or militiamen). Unfortunately, they would find that Spartacus's forces had greatly increased. It is believed the gladiator general was now in command of more than four thousand people, and he was ready and waiting for Varinius and his generals.

Not only did Spartacus have more men than the praetor expected, but the slave army also had the tactical advantage, as they were very familiar with the terrain. Varinius and his Roman troops trudged through the damp fall weather toward Vesuvius, and along the way, they found another enemy amongst their ranks. As they marched, many of Varinius's soldiers began falling ill, and that, combined with loyalty issues amongst his ranks, would play a big part in his final defeat. On top of this, like many of the Roman praetors who were sent to quell the slave uprisings, Varinius looked at his enemies as weak and unworthy of meeting him on the battlefield. Spartacus was aware of the disdain the Romans held for him and his fellow slaves, and he intended to decimate any Roman forces that he came up against.

The Roman praetor first sent out Furius with his squadron of two thousand men to meet Spartacus near the base of Vesuvius. Furius's men were easily decimated by the slave forces. Spartacus had men constantly surveilling the areas near the mountain, so he was also able to locate another party of Roman troops that intended to attack him. Caught off-guard, Cossinius and his men fought bravely, but they were able to overcome their attackers. Those left alive, including Cossinius himself, fled. The Romans were unable to grab all of their equipment and supplies because of the sudden attack, so Spartacus and his men seized everything that had been left behind before giving chase.

It didn't take Spartacus and his soldiers long to catch up with the Romans, and eventually, the majority of the Roman soldiers were overpowered and killed by the slave army, including Cossinius. With the praetor's lieutenants easily dispatched, Spartacus turned his army to the south and continued to add to his ranks as he traveled.

Varinius was unwilling to take this defeat, so he marched his troops southward as well, running straight into Spartacus's forces in Lucania. Spartacus and his men were already in battle formation, and upon seeing this, many of the praetor's men refused to attack. Some of them even fled. Undeterred by the dissension in his ranks, Varinius pushed on with his remaining men. To the Roman praetor's surprise, the men that he met on the battlefield were better trained and more focused than he had anticipated.

The troops led by Spartacus ripped through the Roman forces with inhuman strength and speed. Varinius watched as his men fell, slaughtered by those he thought were beneath him. Upon seeing this, he turned to retreat. But as the Roman praetor turned, he came face to face with the gladiator general and was soon felled from his horse. Although Varinius was not mortally wounded, he lost his prized horse and had to flee for his life.

Spartacus wanted to take this humiliation one step further in order to avenge the loss of one of his fellow leaders, Oenomaus. He took the captured legionnaires and delivered punishments that seemed fitting to him. Many of these men were put in an arena and made to fight to the death, a fate that would have awaited him and his fellow gladiators. For those who didn't receive this punishment, Spartacus chose Rome's favorite form of punishment: crucifixion. This ultimate humiliation made its way to the ears of the Roman Senate, and they finally realized they had to take the threat more seriously.

Spartacus and his men continued to raid and attack Campania, destroying whatever Roman forces were left there by Varinius. This meant decimating the Roman forces left under the control of Gaius Thoranius, Varinius's quaestor. As Spartacus continued his raiding of the southern regions of Italy, his forces continued to grow. Though there were many skirmishes during the winter months of 73 BCE and the early part of 72 BCE, Spartacus mostly focused on training the men and finding ways to equip and supply the ever-growing ranks of their army.

By this point, Spartacus's slave army had accrued several wins over the mighty Roman military, but those battles had been against mostly untrained and inexperienced soldiers. The gladiator general knew that his forces weren't ready to stand up against the more seasoned soldiers who were bound to come their way. For this reason, he put forth the idea of marching to the Alps, which were well out of the range of Rome's more experienced forces. However, he wasn't the only leader amongst the rebellious slaves, and Crixus stepped forward with his own plan. The Gallic warrior was bolstered by the recent victories against the Roman militia, and he believed that they should use this momentum and head straight for the serpent's head: Rome.

The two contradicting strategies left the bulk of the slave army divided. Unable to come to some sort of compromise, the two leaders broke ties and followed their own paths. Crixus took thirty thousand men (this included a small group of Germanic and Gallic gladiators) and broke away, looking to not only march on Rome but also to continue raiding the villages and towns of southern Italy.

With this division of the slave forces, Rome could no longer scoff at the slave uprising as a simple outbreak of disobedience. The spring of 72 BCE would see two more Roman generals attempt to disband the slave army. These Roman generals were given command of four legions in order to complete this mission. The first of these commanders to see battle was Lucius Gellius.

Gellius had begun achieving his political ambitions at a young age; he spent his youth climbing up the ladder until he was eventually elected as a quaestor in 102 BCE. Still hungry for more, the young man continued to look for more responsibility, and this led him to the position of aedile (these individuals were appointed to maintain public buildings and regulations during public festivals) in 96 BCE. He would continue his climb until he found himself a consulate in 72 BCE, where he aligned himself with Gnaeus Pompeius Magnus (better known as Pompey or Pompey the Great). Gellius was eventually given control of a sizable force by the Senate, which expected him to easily take care of the slave revolt.

Spartacus may have been more challenging for this general to find, but Crixus and his forces were making their presence well known, as they were raiding and rampaging through the small cities and towns of southern Italy. Thus, Lucius Gellius opted to start with this faction of the slave rebellion. He sent two of his legions to the

Apulia region (an area in the southeastern corner of Italy) to deal with the rebel gladiator. Leading these forces was the praetor Quintus Arrius, who was to become the next governor of Sicily. However, before doing so, he had to take care of Crixus and Spartacus. Gellius believed that the praetor could march fast enough to lock the gladiator and his army in place with the ocean to their back, so he was confident that his forces would be able to rout this portion of the slave army.

The Roman forces were indeed able to make good time and keep their presence relatively unknown. Near Mount Garganus, the Romans mounted a surprise attack on Crixus and his forces. Crixus and his men found themselves boxed in, and they had to fight ferociously to escape. Unfortunately, they were no match for the Roman legions that they met on the battlefield, and more than half of Crixus's men were cut down. Tragically, amongst the death toll was Crixus himself. Once word of his friend's demise reached Spartacus, he was enraged. While the massacre of his fellow gladiator and his men had been going on, Spartacus had set up camp in the Apennines (the mountain range that runs through the center portion of southern Italy, from the tip of the boot to the top of the leg).

Spartacus spent the winter months training and building up their supplies. He spent a lot of time sending his men out on foraging missions in the surrounding area. These missions included plundering estates and towns and looking for horses to build a better calvary. Spartacus knew that having a well-trained and extensive cavalry could make a major impact in his battles with the Roman forces. It would also make his army's trek to and through the Alps much easier. As Spartacus's men ransacked towns like Consentia (modern-day Cosenza), their ranks grew as well, as more and more slaves were freed from their oppressors. By the time the winter had ended, Spartacus had amassed around seventy thousand people in his army. These slaves, if capable, were given weapons and trained in combat.

As winter began to thaw into spring, Spartacus and his army began moving north, with both Gnaeus Cornelius Lentulus Clodianus and Lucius Gellius hot on his trail. Clodianus had set up north of the gladiator's camp and was hoping to meet Spartacus on his way into the Cisalpine region. The consul, much like his partner in this mission, Lucius Gellius, found himself aligned with Pompey. Having served under him in Hispania, Clodianus had gained his favor and eventually used these connections to be elected as a praetor in 75 BCE. Keeping his eye on the prize, Clodianus was eventually put into the position of consul in 72 BCE. He would then work to bring about Pompey's interests in the Hispania region of the republic until he was called upon to join forces with Gellius to combat Spartacus and his rebellion.

Lucius Gellius, who had dealt with Crixus in the south, looked to take Spartacus from behind while Clodianus blocked Spartacus from moving any farther north. The two consuls hoped to trap Spartacus in the middle, which would allow them to overrun him more easily. As Gellius moved from the south, he came upon a small group of Spartacus's horses that had found themselves cut off from the rest. Some of the slave warriors had drifted away from the main body of the army and were quickly surrounded and decimated by Gellius and his Roman legions as they moved north to meet Spartacus's main forces.

Clodianus chose to utilize the same course of action as Gellius had in the south with Crixus and set about attempting to surround Spartacus and his men. But Spartacus's numbers were far superior, and he turned his forces on Clodianus's legions, attacking them without delay. This maneuver was unexpected and threw the general off-balance, leaving Spartacus with the upper hand. Attacking ferociously and without mercy, Spartacus eradicated a large majority of the Roman soldiers, and this threw Clodianus into a panic, causing the remainder of the troops to retreat.

By the time the battle had ended, Gellius's troops had closed in on Spartacus's rear flank. By turning his forces around and utilizing the same strategies as he had with Clodianus, Spartacus was able to defeat Gellius as well. Without a new plan of attack, the Roman consul fled. Spartacus and his forces were able to capture more than three hundred Roman prisoners. Just as before, he sentenced some of them to fight in gladiatorial combat until the death. He crucified the others, all in the name of honoring his fallen brethren Crixus.

In the meantime, the two consuls would regroup and begin planning their next offensive against the expanding slave army. To do this, the two consuls fled to Rome, where they recruited more men for their armies. Realizing that they were unable to defeat the gladiator general on their own, the two consuls then merged their forces and moved to meet Spartacus on a new battlefield.

Spartacus was undeterred from his prior mission and marched his troops toward the Alps. As he traveled, more and more slaves and gladiators, as well as shepherds and other peasants, joined his ranks. It is believed that there were about 120,000 people following Spartacus as he marched into Cisalpine Gaul (northern Italy).

But when they reached the city of Mutina, they were greeted by the governor of the region, Gaius Cassius Longinus, and ten thousand men. Cassius had just been placed in power as the proconsul of the region after spending several years working his way up the ranks of the Roman elite. The governor had little to no experience on the battlefield, so he kept close to the Roman praetor Gnaeus Manlius. The two rode out to meet the slave horde, but they were no match for Spartacus and his men. Spartacus and his mighty slave army overtook Cassius and his men, killing most of them. Cassius and a handful of men were somehow able to escape the Battle of Mutina with their lives.

The path to the Alps was now completely free of obstacles, but after having tasted so much success, many of Spartacus's men fell back, believing, as Crixus had, that the true route to utter victory involved taking their fight straight to Rome. And it seems that Spartacus may have agreed with them. While it is not known for sure why Spartacus didn't cross the Alps, it is likely that he believed he could take on Rome or that he wanted to prevent dissension in the ranks or the division of his forces. Regardless, Spartacus abandoned his plan and turned south to march on Rome. In order to make this march easier on him and his men, Spartacus ordered his men to kill any remaining prisoners and any excess pack animals to lighten the army's load.

It was one thing for this band of slaves and gladiators to have beaten militiamen and untrained generals, but the slaves inflicting defeats against such well-thought-of Roman generals as Lucius Gellius and Gnaeus Cornelius Lentulus Clodianus was a crushing blow to the Roman Republic. The Senate now knew it had to do something drastic. However, Rome was experiencing a shortage of generals and men, as many of them were stationed in outlying regions of the republic, like Spain and Asia Minor. With no sitting Roman military commander close at hand, the Senate had to look within the ranks of the elites for someone they felt had enough prowess to defeat Spartacus. For this, they turned to Marcus Licinius Crassus, who was a wealthy landowner and had learned much under the tutelage of the Roman general Sulla (Lucius Cornelius Sulla Felix) years prior. That, coupled with Crassus's lineage, made him the perfect choice.

Marcus Licinius Crassus had been born with a bright future, as he was a part of one of the most respected families in Rome. He inherited the family fortune after tragedy struck his older brother and father; he also married his brother's wife, a circumstance that was unique even back then.

However, Crassus's family had supported Sulla during his civil war. Although Sulla was victorious, he left Rome, which was retaken by the opposition. The Roman Senate then placed proscriptions on those who had supported Sulla. In order to get out of these punishments, Crassus fled to Hispania. He called this region home for several years before moving on to Greece, where he eventually found a position in Sulla's army during his second civil war. Crassus, along with other men, such as Pompey, found fame while learning the art of war under the mighty Roman general.

After returning home to Rome, he found that all of his family's lands and wealth had been auctioned off. Crassus quickly set about working on rebuilding his family's reputation and wealth. He also had many other interests, such as developing the first Roman fire brigade and working on building a political career. His dedication and determination paid off with the Senate's appointment of him as the head of the Roman legions. And it wasn't long before intel reached Crassus's desk that informed him that Spartacus was nearing Picenum. (The gladiator had been utilizing the central Adriatic coast to work his way toward Rome.)

Crassus rolled out and set up camp at the borders of the region and waited for Spartacus and his army to reach them. Cassius ordered one of his lieutenants, Marcus Mummius, to take two legions and position himself a distance behind the slave army and hold that position until otherwise instructed. Mummius was also born into a wealthy family, and he was looking to gain favor politically as well as militarily.

Due to this sentiment, he disregarded the orders of his superior, as he felt he had an opening that could lead to a victorious defeat of Spartacus and his men. Charging forward, the lieutenant and his men were easily pushed back, and he lost many of his men during the battle. Crassus didn't sit idly by while Mummius was being attacked; he urged some of his men on to assist the lieutenant in his ill-advised attack. In order to not lose all of them, Mummius ordered his men to throw down their weapons and retreat. This gave Spartacus another opportunity to build his supplies, and it ended up being a disastrous and humiliating defeat for Mummius.

Mummius returned to the ranks of Crassus's legion, where he was received with disappointment and anger. Crassus quickly rearmed the remaining soldiers of the defeated legion and instructed them to give a solemn oath that they would never drop their weapons again. But this slap on the wrist could not be the only consequence for the legion. To prove a point, Crassus gathered together five hundred of the men (most of whom were identified as those who had fled first) and had them divide into fifty ten-man groups. The groups were then instructed to draw lots, and the one that came up short would be executed on the spot. All of the legions were forced to watch this, as it was a clear message of what Crassus intended to do to any legionnaire who decided to be disobedient or a coward.

Now that his men understood what discipline was, Crassus set about retraining and rearming those troops he had left. He wanted to make sure that every one of his legionnaires was adept with the short sword, and he also began training them with the spear as well. Along with this training, he reorganized his legions into groups of 480 men, which would make it easier for Crassus to strategically maneuver the men over the battlefield. By the time these preparations were done, Crassus stood in front of eight well-trained legions. He had full confidence that they would pursue and eradicate Spartacus and his slave army. With this, Crassus marched after Spartacus.

It is possible that after his victory at the Battle of Picenum, Spartacus thought he had seen a difference in the Roman forces. Perhaps he thought that his troops were not ready to take Rome on. However, this is just a theory; it is not known exactly why Spartacus left Rome untouched. Even though he was only kilometers away from the city, he decided to take his troops south, where he continued raiding and plundering the Italian countryside. Eventually, he would take the town of Thurii, and he would treat this city almost as if it was his capital. Spartacus's army then marched into the Lucania region, experiencing many small defeats along the way.

With Crassus hot on his trail, the gladiator general found himself in Bruttium (located in the toe of Italy) and then found his way to Rhegium (a coastal city on the mainland that was not far from Messana—modern-day Messina—on Sicily). Spartacus thought Sicily might be the perfect location to set up a more permanent camp. After all, Sicily had been home to the previous two slave rebellions, so Spartacus likely felt there would be kindred spirits on the island who could help build an even larger army and set Rome ablaze.

But the only way to cross the Strait of Messana (Messina) without utilizing Roman ships was to barter with the Sicilian pirates. Spartacus had some wealth by this point, as he had spent months raiding estates. He was soon able to find some Sicilian pirates and offered to pay them to ferry thousands of men to Sicily. Spartacus, though, would find out the bitter sting of betrayal, as the pirates who had taken the money and agreed to the contract failed to show up at the rendezvous point.

Of course, this left Spartacus and his gladiator army in a very poor position. Crassus acted quickly and reworked his strategy. Instead of facing the large slave army on the battlefield, Crassus opted to build a wall that would corner Spartacus on the peninsula. This wall would allow Crassus to not expend any supplies or men but rather wait for the slave army to be starved into submission.

According to Plutarch, the famed Greek historian, the Roman commander instructed his legions to dig a fifteen-foot-wide ditch across a thirty-five-mile stretch of land. Once that was done, then wood and stone were used to create a wall.

Spartacus was annoyed by the construction of this wall, but he continued looking for another way to get his troops out of this predicament. Afraid that he would be unable to conquer the wall, Spartacus sent word to Crassus that he was ready to enter into peace negotiations. But Crassus took this as a sure sign that his plan was working and rejected the slave general's offer. This left Spartacus back in the same position he was in, and that meant he had to figure out how to overcome the Romans' strategy.

Winter approached rapidly, and Spartacus and his army were running low on supplies. The gladiator general knew that the only way to get out of this predicament was to go through the wall, and for this to happen, he had to devise a strategic plan. Spartacus and his men waited for night to fall on one winter evening, and when the visibility was low due to a winter storm, they stealthily found a small section of the ditch and filled it with wood and earth. After creating a bridge across the ditch, Spartacus and his forces then battered down the wall, freeing themselves from the siege.

The slave army rapidly moved into Lucania, and this move sent waves of panic throughout Rome. Crassus's inability to stop the slave army left the Roman Senate feeling that they needed to bolster the legions already combating this menace. They knew their next decision had to be something big, so they sent word to Pompey and Marcus Terentius Varro Lucullus to return home and join forces with Crassus. This created a sense of urgency in Crassus, as he did not want to share any of the glory with other political rivals, let alone Pompey and Lucullus. Both of these Roman commanders had seen widespread success in several different campaigns. Lucullus had gained quite a reputation through his career; he had been in Macedonia when he was recalled back to Italy. Pompey had done the same with his campaigns in Hispania.

The long winter and the seashore took their toll on the gladiator army, and cracks began to appear within the command. A large band of men chose to splinter from Spartacus and follow two Gallic warriors named Gannicus and Castus. This new faction set up camp in a small area near a lake in Lucania. Hearing word of this dissension, Crassus sent around six thousand men to the location and instructed them to take the high ground. They were to do this before the slaves could do so and to do it quietly so as not to alert their enemies. However, the troops were unable to complete that portion of the mission, as they were seen. Learning of this, Crassus had to act quickly, and he rushed into the battle that had broken out. The battle was furious and fast, but the rebellious slave army stood their ground and held off the Roman soldiers until Spartacus could arrive with reinforcements. Even with these reinforcements, Crassus and his Romans legions were able to slaughter over twelve thousand of the faction's men.

Spartacus and his army retreated toward the area surrounding Petelia, looking to set up a defensive camp in the mountains. Knowing that he had delivered a devastating blow, Crassus sent two of his lieutenants and several legions to pursue Spartacus. Scrophas and Quintus took their men and executed several attacks on the rear flanks of Spartacus's army. Knowing that he would never make it to his planned destination without shaking the legions trailing behind him, Spartacus quickly turned his forces around and attacked the legions head-on. Once again, this strategic move threw the Roman legions off-kilter, and the furious battle ended with the Roman forces being decimated. Many of the Roman legionnaires were cut down in battle. Scrophas was rescued by his men; he barely made it out of the battle alive.

When the slave army heard that reinforcements led by Pompey and Lucullus were arriving, they knew it would make a bad situation even worse. At the same time, though, Spartacus's army was once again energized by the stunning defeat they had just given to the Roman legions. Regardless, Spartacus still felt the best plan of action was to move to the high ground and build a defensive line. However, his generals and his army were unwilling to retreat any farther. Instead, they urged their leader to arm everyone once again and march headlong into the oncoming Roman legions. Some of Spartacus's leaders also felt that the better plan would be to move south to Brundisium, where they could hire a merchant ship and escape the mainland to recollect themselves before attempting another run at Rome. The slaves' uncertainty played right into Crassus's hands, as he wanted to end the conflict before his rivals could reach the region so that he could gain all the glory of taking down Spartacus and the slave rebellion.

But unfortunately, that plan, though sound, would be thwarted by the fact that Lucullus and his legions landed at that very city and began moving inland to meet up with Crassus and his men. Spartacus was trapped between two armies, as well as another approaching one, but he still attempted to refrain from battle as much as possible.

Crassus somehow found his way into close proximity of the gladiator army's camp and prepared for what he deemed would be the final battle. Once again, the Roman commander sent orders to several of his men to begin digging a trench around the slave encampment. The slave army soon caught wind of this, and many of them began jumping into the ditch and attacking the Roman soldiers. As more and more of the slave soldiers sprang to action, Spartacus knew that conflict would not be avoided, and so, choosing the lesser of three evils, he pulled his soldiers together and moved on Crassus.

After having called for battle, Spartacus's men brought him his horse, and in an act of defiance, the gladiator drew his weapon and struck it down. By doing this, he made it clear that there was no other choice but to fight until they had no breath left or until every Roman soldier was under their boot. The mighty slave army rushed forward, outnumbering the Roman legions by many. They ran straight into the legions' wall of shields and experienced swords.

Having been repelled initially, Spartacus gathered his troops together once again and advanced forward.

Swords and bodies were falling left and right, and Spartacus was determined to meet the leader of this legion one on one, so he made his way through soldiers and bodies until he saw Crassus across the field, sitting on top of a small hill and watching the battle from a distance. Spirited on by the sight of his rival, Spartacus pushed through, killing legionnaire after legionnaire, but he was never able to make it to the Roman commander himself. Unfortunately for Spartacus, his legend preceded him. When several of the legionaries saw who he was, they turned and encircled him.

Spartacus had been struck several times on his push through the mass of men on his mission to clash swords with Crassus, but even though he had suffered many injuries, the proud Thracian warrior stood his ground. Supposedly, as the Roman legionnaires swarmed upon him, he continued fighting until the last breath left his body. (It should be noted, though, that his body was never recovered, but most historians assume he died in this battle.)

Crassus had done what no other Roman general and commander had been able to do. He had completely annihilated the bulk of the gladiator army. Though many of Spartacus's men fled the battle and found refuge in the hills, the bulk of his forces were wiped out. However, Crassus had also taken quite a beating, which means it was up to the other Roman commanders to track down the remaining fugitive slaves.

Pompey used this to elevate his role in the annihilation of the slave army by routing as many of the slaves as possible. Pompey, Crassus, and Lucullus killed or captured over ten thousand slaves. Now all that was left for Crassus and his legions was to triumphantly return to Rome along the Appian Way. This road was an ancient route that had been used to transport military supplies since 312 BCE. Taking this road into the capital not only made the march easier but also made a statement. As Crassus and the other generals marched along the Appian Way, they would be visible by many people. This allowed the victorious commander to send a message to the remaining slaves and lower-class Roman citizens as he traveled to Rome.

Crassus supposedly captured six thousand slaves, who he crucified on the road to Rome. The Roman commander would stop every few feet and order his men to mount a slave and raise them high above the ground. The slaves, who were writhing in pain upon the cross, could be heard for great distances and were left to die so that anyone traveling down the main road into Rome would know what would happen if they dared to stand up or rebel against the Roman Republic. This decisive victory and subsequent punishments ended the Third Servile War and showed many the might of the Roman Republic.

Conclusion

Though undoubtedly every one of the Servile Wars played a part in changing the Roman Republic, the third one may have had the most impact. Without the First and Second Servile Wars, though, there is no telling if the slaves of that gladiator school would have had the courage to stand up and fight.

Sicily was greatly changed by the consequences of the Servile Wars. The Romans realized they had to have a larger presence on the island, so the Roman government opted to increase the urbanization of several of the major cities. This allowed them to have a bigger hold on the island and, therefore, on the slaves within its borders.

Since the Third Servile War took place on the mainland and hit so close to home for the Roman elite, many of whom lived in the capital, it had more of an impact than the other two insurrections. It was the largest of the slave revolts, and it was led by men who were mighty enough to stand up against some of the most well-decorated geniuses of the Roman military. The defeat of Spartacus and his slave army would elevate names like Crassus and Pompey to new heights.

Although Pompey was not involved in the final battle itself, the fact that his legions were able to capture so many of the fleeing warrior slaves would bring him new avenues of power. The actions of Pompey would also create tensions with Crassus and build a lifelong rivalry. Pompey's decision to claim credit for ending the war didn't sit well with Crassus or his supporters.

Though their rivalry was ignited through this conflict, both Pompey and Crassus received a hero's welcome when they returned home to Rome with their men. The two generals wouldn't enter Rome itself. Instead, they chose to keep their legions intact and set up camp on the outskirts of the capital. Their victory against Spartacus allowed them to be put up for consulship in 70 BCE, despite the fact that Pompey was not even eligible for this position due to his age (he was only thirty-five). But because of the mighty victory these two generals had delivered, the Roman Senate elected both as consuls. However, there is some speculation on if the presence of their men outside of the city walls aided them in their political win.

Not only did Spartacus's war affect the political lives of the two men who were able to bring the gladiator to his knees, but it also affected the lands ripped apart by the conflict. Like with the other two Servile Wars, the Third Servile War devastated southern Italy. Towns were razed to the ground, and many of the slaves of these towns and estates, along with the poorer classes, had laid down their tools and picked up weapons in hopes of freedom. This left many of the slaves who were able to escape into the wilderness without any means of survival. Looking for food and money to survive, many of these slaves turned to crime, which left southern Italy rife with bands of criminals.

Economically, the uprising by Spartacus and the subsequent war left many southern Italian landowners struggling financially with properties that either had been completely destroyed or damaged. It took years for them to find their footing again. All of this devastation left the latifundia system of southern Italy in total disarray. These parcels of land that had been once gained through the conquering of local tribes had become privately owned parcels of land that were passed down in families. These estates often raised livestock or cultivated olive oil and wine. Most of these were owned by wealthy Roman elites, but with the new atmosphere of the republic caused by the slave revolts, these upper-class Roman citizens had to come up with a new system.

With the slave shortage, these estate owners chose to find a way to maintain their lands without using slaves. The answer to this problem was renting out portions of their land to individuals who would work it and take care of the livestock. For this, the estate owners would be given rent and a share of the crops, much like the feudal system that would be present in medieval Europe. Even with the shortage of slaves, there were many landowners who still utilized a small group of slaves to ensure that household chores and other menial labor were completed.

Of course, with this change of work distribution, the Roman elite also had to figure out a new way to ensure their slaves were kept under control. This sometimes led to minor rebellious uprisings on individual estates. This is why during this transitional period, it was common to see search parties out in the Italian countryside looking for escaped slaves.

For the most part, though, these estate owners began using fewer and fewer slaves and instead offered a small wage to freemen in order to ensure that all of their crops were maintained and harvested. Overall, many Romans' views on slaves themselves were altered with the rise of Spartacus. After all, Spartacus had been a slave and yet had had many of the attributes and virtues that Roman citizens held in high regard. On top of this, the Roman emperors who followed in the coming centuries concentrated more on building the empire they had rather than expanding it any further. This meant a decreased influx of slaves, which left estate owners having to look at hiring laborers rather than purchasing slaves who had been captured.

This new outlook and the shortage of slaves also impacted the legal rights of those still held as slaves. Beginning with Emperor Claudius, new laws were put in place during the Roman Empire that elevated the protection of slaves. The first of these laws to be enacted stated that any slave owner who murdered an elderly or sickly slave would be charged with murder. This law also stated that if an elderly or sickly slave was not provided any assistance, they automatically earned freedom. More laws were to come that would increase the rights of slaves. Many of these built upon the idea that slave owners would be held responsible for the mistreatment and murder of their slaves.

For centuries after the Third Servile War, laws on slaves began to change and expand. Many historians and experts agree that the conflict and the subsequent devastation of the lands that came about definitely played a part in igniting the flame of more rights for slaves. Though the extent of this may never be known, there was a marked decrease in slave ownership in the Roman Empire. On top of this, the perception of slavery began changing drastically, and the Roman leaders and elites worked hard to ensure that such an uprising never happened again. In fact, the Third Servile War not only was the largest of the slave uprisings, but it was also the last major one in both the Roman Republic and Roman Empire.

Part 2: Spartacus

A Captivating Guide to the Thracian Gladiator Who Led the Slave Rebellion Called the Third Servile War against the Roman Republic

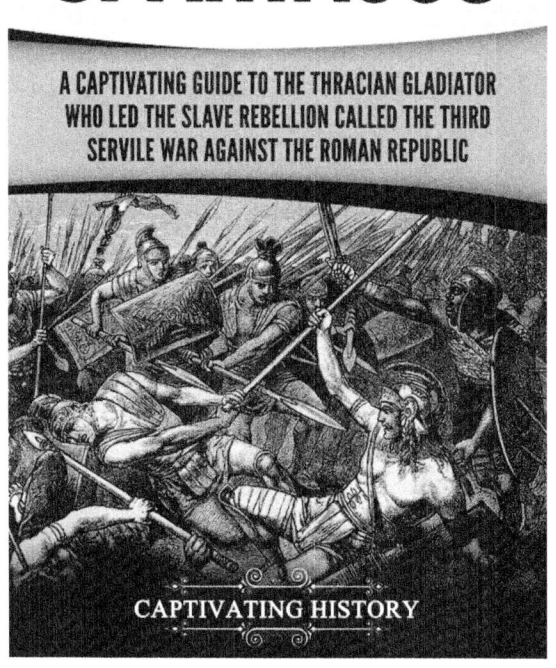

Death is the only freedom a slave knows. That's why he's not afraid of it. That's why we'll win.

From the 1960 Stanley Kubrick film, *Spartacus*

Introduction

Almost 2,100 years ago, a gladiator walked out of the arena. And he never walked back into it.

Spartacus, a Thracian whose early life is hidden in the mists of history, is one of the most infamous figures of antiquity. Perhaps the most famous gladiator of all, parts of Spartacus' story inspired elements of the award-winning film *Gladiator* (2000). Yet even though his story is familiar to millions, he remains a strangely mysterious figure, one whose innermost heart was never revealed to the world. All of the existing records about Spartacus and the war that he started and lost were written by Roman historians. None of the slaves' account of these events has survived the onslaught of the years; thus, many of Spartacus' actions, and all of his motives, are matters of speculation. Even Plutarch, a contemporary, could only guess at what this hero of the oppressed truly wanted or how he really felt. Diving into this great man's psyche and puzzling together his thoughts and feelings is a fascinating subject. And his story makes for gripping reading.

Born a free man—possibly even a prince—he had become a mercenary for the Romans. Then he'd been a deserter, a bandit, and an insurgent. When they caught him, he became a prisoner. And then they sold him as a slave.

At the so-called "school" (really more of a prison) at Capua, Spartacus became a gladiator. All his life, he had known how to fight for food, resources, and survival. Now, the Romans forced him to fight for their entertainment. It was either fight his fellow slaves or die at their blades, and *fight or die* became the single rule by which Spartacus' life was lived. Shackled at night in a dark and lonely cell and participating by day in a blood sport that could kill him at any second, always at the whim of his master, Spartacus had become one of the most miserable slaves in history.

He lived a slave, but he would die a hero.

With kitchen knives and sheer guts and determination, Spartacus and a handful of his friends would fight their way out of the school at Capua and go in search of a better life. And so, their journey began, a journey that has captivated the imaginations of millions, from Marxist revolutionaries to novelists and filmmakers. Now, allow Spartacus' story to capture yours.

This story has all the hallmarks of a tale more exciting than history, a tale that comes to life with the excitement of fiction and yet the poignant reality of true events. There are battles and consuls, Romans and Thracians, slaves and the free. There are pirates and gladiators, as well as a jealous praetor seeking to prove himself in the eyes of the public, pitted against a courageous freedom fighter whose only goal is to get back to his homeland. Treachery, greed, power, freedom, ingenuity, and imagination fill this tale, which takes place all the way from the feet of Vesuvius to the mighty rampart of the Alps to the shores of the Strait of Messina.

This is the story of Spartacus. And this book will bring it to you as you've never heard it before.

Chapter 1 – Thrace and Its Enemies

The story of Thrace begins long before history, in the mysterious darkness of a time when writing had not yet been invented. That era is long lost to us, but that is not to say that it was uneventful. People were people then just as they are now, and as now, they were busy: making war, obtaining nourishment, falling in love, searching for a place to call home. And around eight thousand years ago, somewhere around 6000 BCE, a group of Indo-European tribes stumbled upon a land that their people would call home for the next six millennia. Bound by mountains to the east, a great river to the north, and seas on the south and east, this land was one of wild and abundant beauty. Its cascading rivers had carved for themselves great harsh valleys, the landscape plunging down into the roaring expanse of the river. The mountains ran down into great plateaus as wide and wild as the mighty sky, and the seas were glittering blue, warm to the touch, awash with natural resources. With damp, cool winters and hot, dry summers, this land appeared perfect to the tribes who found themselves wandering into its untamed wilderness.

The land was a part of modern-day Bulgaria, Turkey, and Greece, known to history as Thrace, and the peoples who first came to live there were known as the proto-Thracians. They were a group of agricultural tribes who tilled the fertile earth and raised animals on the rich grazing lands, and soon, this little handful of people grew up into a vast nation. "Thrace" was not their own name for their country. In fact, what the Thracians called themselves has been lost to the mists of time; the name was bestowed upon them by the Greeks.

But for thousands of years, the Greeks stayed in Greece, and the Thracians of Thrace were free to explore and tend to their crops and animals in the rich abundance of their beautiful surroundings. Most of what we know about Thracian culture comes from archaeological findings; the first written record of Thrace is a vague reference in Homer's *Iliad*, and it was only in 450 BCE that Herodotus would thoroughly document these people. It would appear, however, that despite their simple lives in small rural villages, the Thracians had a rich and fascinating culture. They loved poetry and music, although none of it survived to this day. They were also polygamists and believed in the afterlife, having elaborate burial sites and rituals.

To all appearances, the Thracians thrived. And lacking any oppressor to force them into unity, they began to squabble with one another. As the centuries slipped by, the Thracians continued to make war among themselves. These wars made their young men strong and nimble, developing weapons and armor that was unrivaled among the neighboring countries and regions. Living in villages instead of cities, these men became outstanding guerilla warriors as they fought each other, relying on their sharp wits, knowledge of the landscape, and excellent equipment. The Thracians carried crescent-shaped wicker shields, javelins, and a large dagger known as a *sica*, which was made of steel. They were quick on their feet and mobile, moving effortlessly through the rugged landscape to wage war on each other over land, resources, and power.

Historians have reflected that it was a pity the Thracians chose to pit themselves against each other instead of against the neighboring Greeks and Macedonians. Such was their military prowess that they may well have been able to conquer their neighbors and build an empire of their own. Instead, every time a threat arose from beyond their borders, the Thracians were too busy fighting each other to stand against their enemies as one united force. The Thracians could probably have beaten anyone in a war if they had only been able to bring themselves to peace. But they never did.

Around 700 BCE, the ancient Greeks began to colonize Thrace fairly peacefully. The Greeks became a profound influence on Thrace and its people, and they also became the first people to write about the Thracians, describing them as fearless fighters. Greek armies at the time were largely made up of hoplites, slow-moving foot soldiers burdened with heavy spears and shields. Greek generals decided that the Thracians would be ideal additions to their army, and so, they hired thousands of them as mercenaries. These mercenaries became known as peltasts.

In the early 6th century BCE, Persia, under King Darius the Great, swept across the Balkans and attacked. The Thracians could not find the unity to fight them, and as such, their country was incorporated into the mighty Achaemenid Persian Empire. Darius made their soldiers a vital part of his conquests, and they were wildly successful. With the help of the Thracians, he conquered most of Europe and almost all of Thrace, expanding his empire all the way to the shores of the Black Sea. It should be noted that while some Thracian tribes joined Darius, others decided to stand against him; these forces were annihilated.

But the Persian Empire, despite Darius' brilliance as a commander, was a shooting star: staggering while it lasted but very brief. The Achaemenid Empire went into decline after his rule, and in the 5th century BCE, Thrace made one great attempt to stand together. Forty of its two hundred tribes came together to build a kingdom known as the Odrysian Kingdom, and for a brief and wonderful period, the world was given a glimpse of what Thrace could have been. It became a much larger territory and grew in power to the point that Thracians now hired Greek mercenaries, with the heavy hoplites complementing the quick peltasts. Xenophon, the famed Greek writer and historian, was one of them.

The Odrysian Kingdom was mighty, but a man arose who was mightier still: Alexander the Great. His father, Philip II, was the first Macedonian who made a mostly successful bid to conquer Thrace; Alexander finished the job in the spring of 335 BCE, and the Odrysian Kingdom was obliterated. Thrace would never again find the unity that had given it almost a century of power. The people that had been conquerors were now merely conquests, with the victorious army broken up and hired out as mercenaries for the Macedonians.

Macedonia's great enemy thus became Thrace's great enemy, and like those that had gone before, this new power would be quick to use Thrace's human resources. This power was ancient Rome—the late Roman Republic, to be exact (it would only become an empire in the first century BCE). At the Battle of Pydna in 168 BCE, Macedonia and Rome faced off against one another. It was a terrible defeat for Macedonia, despite their superior numbers. Rome butchered about 31,000 out of their 43,000 men; by contrast, only 100 Romans fell that day. Macedonia's power was no more, and Rome slowly began to occupy Thrace.

Rome had been in existence for hundreds of years, and since the beginning, slaves had been a part of the city and its growing territories. There was hardly a part of Rome's famed culture that was not built on the backs of men and women who worked without rights, without wages, and without justice. They were in every industry: public works, war, manufacturing, farming, and mining.

Mining was among the worst. Trapped in suffocating darkness, their way lit only by the smoky and flickering glow cast by torches, these slaves were left to dig through the hearts of mountains like helpless worms.

Some of the slaves who lived in sumptuous luxury in Roman palaces had it far worse than even the miners, however. Sex slaves, many of them children, abounded in Rome. For these children, molestation was a daily occurrence, and some would be castrated.

Even the poorest of Romans could afford a slave or two, with the rich owning hundreds. Many of these slaves had been born in their masters' homes, as the child of a slave woman was, by default, a slave as well. Others were procured through more violent means. Prisoners of war, except for those of the highest status, automatically became slaves. Those who were unable to pay their debts would also be enslaved, and very poor families would sometimes sell their own children into slavery.

The most notorious source of slaves was piracy. While the pirates of the Caribbean may have been immortalized in film, the pirates of the ancient Mediterranean were hardly any less fearsome. Under Rome's very nose, they harried the surrounding shores, making their homes close to or even within Roman territory. At the time of Roman Thrace, these pirates inhabited western Cilicia, on the southern coast of modern-day Turkey. And they ran rampant. Stealing, killing, and kidnapping at will, these pirates could have been crushed within Rome's iron fist at any time—except they weren't. Rome needed them. The truth was that these Cilician pirates captured thousands of slaves each year and brought them to Italy to be sold cheaply. Piracy was Rome's most readily available source of slaves, and as long as the Cilician pirates supplied slaves to feed the insatiable appetite for human resources that belonged to a growing power, they would be allowed to wreak havoc in relative peace.

While the Roman Empire had an overwhelming number of slaves, it was the Roman Republic in which they suffered the most. Here, slaves were a dime a dozen, thanks to the overwhelming number of wars that Rome was waging with the Gauls, Britons, and Parthians, to name but a few. The influx of prisoners of war was more than enough to keep Rome supplied with slaves, and because they were so cheap, their masters treated them brutally. What did it matter if a slave died? They could be easily replaced.

Culturally, slaves were so much a part of the Roman world that their presence—and, in the Roman Republic, the harsh treatment of them—was wholly unquestioned. It would only be many years later that slaves would become a contentious issue; in the 2nd century BCE, they were simply a matter of fact. Roman thinking had molded itself so completely around slavery that it would never be questioned. In fact, it would only end when the Roman Empire itself fell in the 8th century CE.

Some of the slaves, however, did aspire for a better life. It is hard to imagine that any of them wouldn't; even those living in luxury were subject to their master's every whim. Yet it was only rarely that they would take action on a large scale, resulting in what became known as the Servile Wars.

The first two Servile Wars took place within forty years of one another. The first, taking place between 135 and 132 BCE, was led by Eunus, a Scythian slave who claimed to receive visions from the gods. In a Joan of Arc-esque uprising, he rallied tens of thousands of slaves in Sicily and attempted to build a city and state of his own. For three years, it looked as though he would succeed, but the Roman army eventually conquered Eunus' army and dragged him off to prison, where illness claimed his life.

The Second Servile War, which took place between 104 and 103 BCE, also took place in Sicily. Consul Gaius Marius had around 800 Italian slaves of the region freed, which sowed discontent among non-Italian slaves, causing them to rise up against their masters. Salvius, who was also a slave, decided to make a bid for what Eunus had come so close to achieving. He led thousands of well-armed troops against Rome, yet his attempt was even shorter-lived. Marius' successors, Quintus Servilius Caepio and Gaius Atilius Serranus, put a stop to the revolt within a year, but it was no easy task.

Yet despite the Servile Wars, there was no question in Roman minds that slavery was simply a part of their culture and would never be changed. So, the pillaging of human freedom went on, with hundreds of thousands of slaves daily carrying out the wills of their masters, their voices drowned out, their faces forgotten.

Rome's consuls and emperors might be some of the most familiar names in history, but it was regiments of slaves who built their empire. Most of these slaves were nameless and faceless, their identities lost forever as irrelevant.

All except for one. And his name was Spartacus.

Chapter 2 – On the Romans' Side

Little is known about the early life of one of history's greatest heroes. The Thracians did not keep much in the way of written records, and they certainly did not keep any records of who could possibly have been a rather inconsequential young man who was born among them. He may have been from the Maedi tribe, a Thracian group known for their nomadic ways. It is vaguely possible that he may have been of royal blood; however, it is more likely that he lived like the majority of the other Thracians had been doing for centuries: in a rural village, roaming the vast plains and rocky crags of his country, tending to livestock.

Even Spartacus' birth year is utterly unknown, although we know he was still a fairly young and definitely very physically capable man when he died in 71 BCE. The estimate most generally accepted for his birth year is 111 BCE, which would have made him about forty when he died.

But that death was a long way away—and practically unimaginable—for the young Spartacus who lived in the land of his ancestors. Roman oppression was as rife in Thrace as anywhere, and as he grew, the young man became more and more aware of what was happening to his people. Just as the Romans were unable to make the crags of the Balkans bow down to them, there was something in the spirit of the Thracians that conquering armies could not extinguish. And it was nowhere stronger than in the heart of Spartacus.

Still, there was little he could do about it, no matter how much it chafed at him that the Romans dictated how his people lived and hired thousands of them to fight their wars. Young and unsure of his future, Spartacus did what most young Thracian men were doing at the time: he joined the Roman military.

There are no records to indicate where Spartacus served or even in which capacity, although due to his lack of Roman citizenship, he would not have served as a legionary. Classical sources mention only the fact that he was a Roman soldier; he was more than likely a mercenary, as most Thracians were, serving in the Auxilia (the auxiliary troops that complemented the much-famed Roman legions). Just as the Greeks had hired the light-footed Thracians to complement their lumbering hoplites, the Romans found these fleet and agile soldiers useful when partnered with their slow legions. Still, one can surmise that Spartacus was a fairly gifted young warrior and that he may have been given some form of command. It was in the Roman army—the army that had conquered vast swathes of the known world—that Spartacus began to learn the art of war. And he learned it well. Thrace had taught him how to fight—warrior's blood coursed through the veins of all young Thracian men—and Rome put that fighting to good work. Spartacus got his first taste of the thrill of hot blood and cold steel meeting, and he also began to learn how to command a group of men, if only by observing how he himself was being commanded. He learned much, and the knowledge would later serve him well. But Roman discipline did not sit well with the Thracian fire in Spartacus' blood.

While Spartacus tried to learn how to balance both fire and steel, hundreds of miles away in Rome, a young man named Marcus Licinius Crassus watched as his family shattered around him.

The political climate of Rome in the early 80s BCE was a stormy one. The Republic of Rome was dying in the childbirth of the Roman Empire. Its unique system of government had served it well for hundreds of years, but the bloated territory was growing too vast to be controlled by consuls. It needed a single, unifying leader whose word was law, but it would still be decades before Julius Caesar became that leader. For now, political intrigue and violence, frequently bordering on civil war, would become rife.

Marcus Licinius Crassus, whether he liked it or not, had been dragged into the mess of Roman politics. Born in 115 BCE, Crassus was raised simply but with an abundant awareness of the power surrounding him. His parents lived in a small home with only a few slaves and no ostentatious displays of power, yet power was something with which the family was very familiar. Crassus' father, Publius Licinius Crassus Dives, was one of Rome's most important figures and a leading military commander, as well as a highly capable and respected politician. When Marcus was only eighteen, Publius had become consul, the highest position that could be held in the Roman Republic; he also served as a commander in modern-day Spain. As Marcus entered adulthood, and despite Publius' and his mother's attempts to raise him thriftily, he learned more than just an acquaintance with power. He learned arrogance.

Marcus' pride would come before a fall. In 88 and 87 BCE, when he was in his late twenties, Rome experienced an upheaval that would change Crassus' life.

From 91 to 88 BCE, Rome had experienced yet another civil war, known as the Social War, when governor Marcus Livius Drusus the Younger intended to grant Roman citizenship to Roman allies living in Italy, which would have tipped the balance of power harshly away from the Roman nobility. His assassination caused the

Roman Republic to erupt into civil war. Gaius Marius, who had been a consul six times and was one of the most ambitious men in Rome, intended to lead the fight against Italy; however, the Senate saw fit to send Lucius Cornelius Sulla Felix instead. Sulla proved to be an outstanding commander, who led Rome to a brisk victory against Italy, and as much as Marius was on the winning side, the victory to him felt more like a defeat. Sulla had proven himself to be Rome's darling, and Marius felt his power was being threatened.

Thus, the battle cries of the Social War of 91-88 BCE had barely begun to fade when they began anew, this time in Sulla's War, which lasted between 88 and 87 BCE. Sulla was determined to grab more power, as his military command had naturally led into a political career. Marius, on the other hand, was extravagantly ambitious, and it is perhaps fitting with Publius' personality that he chose to back Sulla instead. Marcus Crassus joined his father in supporting Sulla, and for a few months, it appeared that they had made the right choice. Marius, then holding more political power, had Sulla kicked out of Rome. However, the slighted general returned with several well-disciplined legions of his own and did the unthinkable: he marched within the city's bounds and meant to attack Rome itself. In all the civil wars the Roman Republic had faced, this move was considered to be unspeakably cruel. Marius had not expected his adversary to deal him so low a blow. He had only a ragtag bunch of gladiators to defend the city, and they fell before Sulla's legions. Sulla took power and became a Roman consul, sending Marius fleeing for his life.

But Marius did not stay down for long. Finding refuge only as far away as distant North Africa, where he fought in the Jugurthine War between Rome and Numidia (modern-day Algeria), Marius began to drum up support thanks to his victory, and it was not a difficult task. Sulla's unethical decision to attack the city of Rome had shaken even his supporters, although Publius and Crassus remained loyal. Driven by a long-ago prophecy that he would become a consul of Rome seven times, Marius was determined to return to Rome and receive his grandiose fate. He was able to put together a more powerful army and marched on Rome just as Sulla had done—and he was even more brutal in his treatment of Sulla's supporters. Over a hundred Roman nobles were butchered for their loyalty to Sulla, and their heads were paraded around the Roman Forum for all to see.

For Rome, this was another wound inflicted on their Republic that was fast being torn apart. For Publius and Crassus, it was a life-changing disaster. Crassus had known little other than stability throughout his young life; now, all of that was going to be uprooted. Publius was found to have supported Sulla, and he was forced to kill himself. Crassus' brother was simply killed. And Crassus had no choice: he had to flee, or he would suffer a similar fate.

His family killed, his home life stripped away from him, and even his pride trampled under the marching feet of Marius' army, Crassus fled like a kicked dog. The only place he could think to go was back to Spain, a long and grueling journey for a young man who had never known want, but at least there he found people who had been his father's allies during his governorship there. They took him in, finding a hiding place for him in a cave by the sea.

So, this was how the 80s BCE found two young men who would someday become the bloodiest of enemies. One, fleet-footed young Spartacus of Thrace, serving in the Roman army and getting his first taste of battle. The other, arrogant Marcus Licinius Crassus of Rome, hiding in a cave overlooking the beating waves. And as Spartacus grew to dislike the Roman legions that had persecuted his people more and more, Crassus gazed out over the foaming sea, alone and afraid. And bitterness grew thick and black in both their hearts.

Chapter 3 – Sold

Illustration I: A contemporary bust of Marcus Licinius Crassus

For eight long months, Crassus sat in that cave, experiencing heat and cold, day and night through the rocky mouth that offered him a view of the ever-changing sea. And in those eight months—fed and watered by an ally who discreetly sent provisions to him every day— Crassus learned about himself. He learned about how much he missed his father. He learned about how badly hardship suited him. And he learned that he never wanted to experience such loneliness, discomfort, and exile ever again.

Meanwhile, Spartacus was probably serving in the Roman army around this time (it is impossible to be certain when exactly he joined, as history's timeline of Spartacus only begins at 73 BCE). But he wouldn't serve for long. He, too, was learning—and mostly what he was learning was that he hated Rome with a fervent passion. Whether he had joined the army for the money or because an honorable discharge would lead to a Roman citizenship and all the privileges that came with it, it was no longer worth it to Spartacus. Something about the Romans must have chafed at him. Maybe it was their history of exploiting Thracians to fight their wars for him. Maybe it was the uncreative discipline of their armies, marching in unison to conquer the world. History cannot tell us of his motives, but for whatever reason, there came a time when Spartacus had abruptly had enough.

So, he did the unthinkable. He deserted.

Deserters were dealt with harshly in Roman times. In fact, most were lucky to simply be banished, their titles and possessions stripped from them as they were driven from the land to fend for themselves. Most were killed, sometimes being clubbed brutally to death by their own comrades once they were captured. Spartacus knew that he was risking death by leaving the Roman ranks, but he decided that living as a free Thracian instead of as a Roman pawn was worth it. In fact, he detested the Romans so much that he became a thorn in their side throughout their expeditions in Thrace and elsewhere, harassing his erstwhile comrades. Some sources say that Spartacus even began to rally support against the Romans from among his own people, working as an insurgent. Others say that he was simply a bandit, attacking the legions to carry off their wealth. It does not seem impossible, given the events that later followed, for the former to have been true. Spartacus had the charisma and the charm necessary to start a rebellion. In fact, if he had been allowed to do this, it is possible that history might have seemed very different. Perhaps if Spartacus had been able to truly rally and unify the wayward Thracians, if he could get them to stand behind his banner and fight the Romans, then Thrace might exist to this day.

But Spartacus never got the chance. His rebellion, if there even was one, never got off the ground because his luck ran out before he could get any further. The Romans captured him once again.

It's not clear why Spartacus wasn't executed for his crime, but his physique likely had something to do with it. The Thracians were a hard and warlike race to start with; Spartacus had been fighting either with or against the greatest army in the world for months. He was mightily strong, a tall figure with rippling muscles that rivaled those of any Roman soldier. Their numbers had overwhelmed him, but they recognized his prowess. Perhaps motivated by money, the Roman commander who had captured Spartacus at last elected not to kill him. He was worth nothing dead, but sold into slavery, Spartacus could make his captor rich.

And so, like Joseph at the hands of his brothers, Spartacus was sold into slavery by the men who had fought alongside him, the men he had left behind. His great strength made him ideally suited to a specific niche in the world of Roman slaves. Spartacus' fate did not include hefting great weights in construction, swinging a pick in a dark mine, or carrying sacks of flour on a mill or farm. Instead, he would do what he had always done. He would fight.

Spartacus became a gladiator.

The Roman gladiator's origins lay beyond Rome itself, back in the distant past when the majority of Italy was populated by a people known as the Etruscans. It was the Etruscans themselves, in fact, who pressured the village of Rome into becoming a place of unity for the tribes they oppressed, thus growing it into a mighty kingdom. After a time, the Etruscans had joined Rome, with some even becoming kings of it before the Roman Republic was born.

Thus, Rome had a strong Etruscan influence on its culture, and perhaps one of the most famous of these influences is the gladiator.

The Etruscans, unlike the Romans, did not use warrior-slaves for entertainment. Instead, they were a part of the Etruscan religion, where they were likely involved with death rites. In fact, when the gladiatorial games first occurred in Rome, they were also a part of the funeral rites of distinguished men. Dozens of slaves belonging to the deceased would fight to the death in a messy and brutal melee as a way of honoring the memory of the warlike dead. The first recorded instance of these slave fights at a funeral occurred in the 3rd century BCE. By the 1st century BCE, these fights were no longer part of the morbid. They were simply entertainment for Rome's yammering masses.

As cultured as Rome could be in its plays, poetry, and music, its entertainment could also be utterly barbaric—and nothing was more so than the gladiatorial games. Gladiators were slaves trained for fighting, and in front of crowds that numbered in the thousands, they would be pitted against one another for the bloodthirsty enjoyment of the audience. While not all the games ended in death, serious injury and mortality were nonetheless very common. And even though the gladiators became to the people of ancient Rome what celebrities are to the modern world, they were still classed as the lowest of the low, with no basic rights and no freedom.

Spartacus had worked with the Romans for long enough to know that this was the fate that awaited him, yet perhaps he was unprepared for the suffering he would endure to get there.

Spartacus was sold to a Roman named Gnaeus Cornelius Lentulus Batiatus, who owned and ran a gladiatorial school in Capua, near modern-day Naples. Little is known about the kind of man that Batiatus was. While the words "gladiator school" conjure up a Hogwarts-esque image with Batiatus as a Dumbledore-like figure, nothing could be further from the truth. This so-called school was no place of wonder and magic: instead, it was little more than a prison. Batiatus and other gladiator trainers like him sought not to empower their gladiators but to make money out of them. A good gladiator was worth a fortune to their owners, and so—physically, anyway—they were well cared for. Fed on fortifying barley to build muscle tone and given only the very best in medical attention, the gladiators were in excellent shape. But they were kept in tiny cells. And, mindful of their physical capabilities and warrior training, their owners kept them in shackles.

For Spartacus, it must have been utterly intolerable. He was not the first Thracian gladiator, nor would he be the last, but like those who had gone before and those who would follow, his heart yearned for the wide skies of Thrace where he had stridden so freely only months before. His wife, classically recorded as a prophetess, had been taken from him. His freedom was gone. All he had now was a dark little cell, with fear and despair radiating off the other gladiators around him, and the prospect of grueling training sessions each morning. Should he refuse to cooperate, he would be whipped or maybe burned with a hot iron—but not badly. Oh, never badly enough to damage the physical body of such a fine specimen of a gladiator. Yet everything about the gladiator school was designed to break his spirit.

Unluckily for Rome, they would soon find that Spartacus' spirit would not be so easy to break.

* * * *

After eight long months in the Spanish cave, news reached Crassus. Gaius Marius had gotten his seventh consulship after all, but he had not enjoyed it for long: he died a short while after receiving the title. Now, Rome was under the control of a Marian consul (supporters of Marius were known as "Marians"), but the passionate fire with which Marius had despised all who supported Sulla had died with him. Crassus was free to escape the cave at last.

He knew better than to go back to Rome just yet, however. Sulla was still alive; in fact, he was campaigning in the east, fighting the First Mithridatic War with the Kingdom of Pontus, wisely staying out of trouble while things settled in Rome. But it was clear to Crassus that Sulla was not done with his attempts to gain power, and Crassus was determined to support him, even if that support had cost his father his life. The death of Publius had fixed Marius and his allies once and for all in Crassus' mind as tyrants. He was going to change that.

Luckily for Crassus, he had plenty of influence on his side in Spain, as many of those subjects were loyal to Publius regardless of who governed Rome. Crassus began to amass wealth and loyalty, aiming to build an army that would eventually march in support of Sulla.

Five years after the death of Publius, in 82 BCE, Crassus finally got to flex his new power. Sulla had emerged from the First Mithridatic War as the decisive victor in 85 BCE and decided it was now time to act. He wrote to the Senate, demanding to be allowed to return home and threatening to do it by force if his request was not granted. The consuls at the time—Marian loyalists named Gnaeus Papirius Carbo and Gaius Marius the Younger, Marius' son—marched to meet him in 82 BCE, and Sulla knew it was time to launch his second civil war. Crassus recognized his chance as well. He took his army and marched to meet Sulla, and he and his men played a vital part in the ensuing battle, which would finally turn the tide. Carbo and Cinna were defeated, and Sulla marched to Rome as its new leader.

The feeling of power and victory were dizzying and wonderful to Crassus. He was no longer a young man, but he had still proven himself in battle against Rome's very best. Even better, Sulla began to purge Rome of Marian loyalists, and their confiscated wealth was distributed among Sulla's favorite allies. Crassus, of course, was among them. His wealth grew enormously, and not only thanks to

Sulla's handouts. Crassus made a name for himself as an astute—and often unethical—businessman. Amassing real estate for low prices (often as the result of a tragedy, such as a fire), Crassus would sell it again for a much greater amount of money. The sound of gold clinking into his coffers proved to be intoxicating to him. Crassus had a reputation for being both generous and extravagant, and he began to prove himself to be dedicated to growing his wealth at all costs. Taking advantage of someone else's tragedy or naivete was his favorite tactic. He was an excellent public speaker and a conniving flatterer, but at his heart, this smooth-talking businessman hid a selfish core.

It was also during his time serving Sulla that Crassus stumbled upon a whole new vice: jealousy. Popular as he was with Sulla, Crassus was not his greatest darling. That title belonged to a young man by the name of Gnaeus Pompeius Magnus, better known as Pompey the Great. Of course, when he and Crassus first got to know each other, Pompey did not yet bear the title of "Magnus" or "Great." It was clear that Pompey was on his way to greatness, though: talented as Crassus was as a military strategist, Pompey far outshone him. That fact chafed hard at Crassus, and where he might otherwise have been content with his money and power, Crassus began to chase after something he lacked: a tremendous military victory. And just like with money, he would stop at nothing to get it.

Chapter 4 – The Real Gladiator

The roar of the crowd was deafening. Spartacus, waiting in the dark, could feel the ground beneath his feet reverberate with the bellowing approval of the Roman crowd. It made his stomach turn. One can imagine that this could have been one of the things he'd hated most about the Roman legionaries who were once his comrades: the thoughtless bloodlust. He could hear the screams out there in the middle of the arena, knew that people were being butchered, people who didn't ask to fight—people who didn't ask to die.

Spartacus hefted his short, angled sword. Its keen edge could part muscle and bone; he'd seen it happen before, watched as skin peeled back from gleaming flesh. Killing was nothing new to him. He was a soldier, after all. But back in the war zone, killing hadn't been accompanied by the roar of the crowd. And the men whose lives he'd taken hadn't been slaves just like him.

It was time to go. Spartacus took a deep breath, shifting the small, rectangular shield on his arm. Some of the other gladiators tried to hang back, fear in their eyes despite the rigorous training they'd all undergone, training that had left scars on their skin. The trainer and his assistants were ready for them, though: waving red-hot irons and swinging whips, they drove the reluctant slaves toward the arena.

Spartacus was a man of war, and he still had his pride to hold on to. He ignored the trainer and walked into the arena of his own accord. When he stepped into the sunlight, it sparkled on the powerful curves of his shoulders and biceps, the defined lines of his pectorals and abdomen. He wore greaves and padding on his legs, as well as a helmet on his head, the metal catching the sun with a brilliance that made the crowd roar. But his torso and arms were utterly bare. His opponents would be forced to strike there—his chest, ribs, lungs, heart, throat—in order to make things more entertaining for the crowd.

This was no real battle. This was entertainment. Yet it was so much more violent than anything that Spartacus had endured on the battlefield.

There was no time for reflection, though. On the other end of the arena, a heavier champion, this time bearing a massive shield and an arrogant sway, was strutting out on the sand. He was a hoplomachus: a heavily armored mockery of the hoplites that the Thracians had once defeated.

Fittingly, Spartacus was a thraex, or Thracian. Once, real Thracians and real hoplites had clashed on the cold mountainsides of Thrace, and only the scream of the wind in the high peaks had accompanied their battle cries. But now as the hoplomachus hefted his shield and screamed, the whole of Rome screamed with him.

Spartacus didn't want to fight him. But just like his opponent, just like those who'd left nothing but bloodstains and drag marks in the sand, he didn't have a choice.

None of them had a choice.

* * * *

There are no records of any of Spartacus' fights in the gladiatorial arena. While fiction has styled him as one of the best, it is unclear whether he even fought at all, although given his military prowess, it is unlikely that he was a mediocre gladiator. We do know much about the lives of the gladiators in general, however—and for all the glory and honor showered upon them, their lives were far from a bed of roses.

Different classes of gladiators bore different kinds of armor and weapons. The murmillo (also spelled as mirmillo or myrmillo) and the hoplomachus were the most heavily armored, but even they had bare torsos like the thraex. Some, like the retiarius, wore no armor at all and didn't even get to carry a "real" weapon: instead, they had fishing nets and tridents and were pitted against gladiators wearing fish-shaped helmets. Spartacus was more than likely a thraex, considering that he really was Thracian. These light-footed, lightly armored gladiators had to fight the heavy hitters, such as the murmillo.

The fights became more and more organized over the years, reaching a point where they had long sets of rules during the Roman Empire. But in the early days—even in the late Roman Republic—they were still crazy skirmishes, a bloody mess that usually led to death. Reluctant though some of the gladiators may have been, they had no choice but to fight. It was either fight or die. Sometimes they wouldn't even fight other humans; instead, caged animals, starved and goaded into crazed ferocity, would be chased into the arena instead. There was no fleeing a boar or a wolf or a bear on the hunt.

It's uncertain for how long Spartacus was a gladiator. By day, he would have been expected to walk into the arena to the cheers of his adoring fans. If he won, he would be showered in palm leaves and money (which, of course, would go straight to his owner). If he lost, he would be expected to show no fear, even in his dying moment, and to conduct himself always with courageous honor.

And by night, he was chained in the dark, kept in a cell, and denied even the right to look up at the stars.

The only bright part of Spartacus' life in the gladiator school was the alliances he managed to forge with his fellow gladiators. During the day, there was no room to talk; there was just training, hours upon hours of it. But at night, when the doors had been bolted and the shackled slaves were left in the darkness, this group of men (and some women) who had been forced to fight for the entertainment of others sought some spark of human contact.

History does not tell us in detail how Spartacus came to know the other gladiators or what their relationships were really like. But considering what came after, their trust in him must have been enormous. Spartacus' radiating charisma, so popular in the gladiatorial arena, did more than simply entertain his fellow slaves outside of it: it inspired them, in a life where inspiration was hard to find. He became well known to the slaves that lived closest to him. Two Gallic gladiators, Crixus and Oenomaus, were particularly close to him. Like Spartacus, they had been taken from wild and beautiful lands that they had once loved and forced to fight in a city they hated. And like Spartacus, they had fire in their blood.

With around 78 gladiators now loyal to Spartacus, the Thracian realized that the time was coming to act. It's uncertain whether Spartacus had plotted a revolt ever since he was first captured or whether life in Capua simply became so unbearable that he saw no other option. Either way, Spartacus made up his mind. He was going to break out of the gladiator school with the help of his 78 comrades. Somehow, he was going to get his freedom back.

In the year 73 BCE, Spartacus and his comrades finally made their move after carefully planning how they were going to escape. They were well-fed, fit, and well-trained fighters, but their weapons were likely kept somewhere inaccessible, probably in a separate building or well-guarded room. Spartacus, though, knew that the armory wasn't the only place where weapons were to be found.

Every day, kitchen slaves brought the gladiators their meals. And there were sharp things in kitchens.

History doesn't tell us how exactly Spartacus and the others managed to get out of their shackles and cells, but they did, and they made a beeline for the kitchen. The kitchen slaves likely fled at the sight of almost 80 brawny gladiators coming at them, giving Spartacus and his men precious moments in which to grab any sharp object they could find, readying themselves for the onslaught of guards that was undoubtedly heading right for them.

It must have been a heart-pounding few minutes in that kitchen, the burly figures of the gladiators yanking open chests and upturning baskets as they hunted for anything that gleamed like metal. But those few minutes were enough. Kitchen knife in hand, Spartacus was ready when the first guard came rushing in. The guards were used to fighting in full armor for money; the gladiators knew how to fought unarmored for nothing but their lives. It was little contest. The gladiators cut down their captors with brutal efficiency and raw fear, and Spartacus led them out of the gladiator school and into the surrounding countryside.

Wounded, breathless, and fully aware that hundreds of Roman soldiers would descend upon them as soon as Batiatus sounded the alarm, Spartacus and his comrades knew that their escape wasn't finished when they stepped out of the gladiator school. Seventy-eight half-dressed, muscular slaves, many of whose faces were easily recognizable from their frequent public appearances, and all wielding some kind of a weapon, could hardly have been more conspicuous if they'd tried. They had to flee somewhere inhospitable, somewhere sparsely populated except perhaps by fellow slaves, and somewhere close enough that they could make it. Spartacus had chosen just the right spot for that purpose.

In 73 BCE, almost 2,100 years ago today, the town of Capua lay at the very feet of a majestic mountain that towered its green and rocky head thousands of feet above the surrounding farmland. Its silent peak was still and beautiful, and it was almost totally void of buildings or people. The climb wouldn't be easy, but Spartacus knew his fit gladiators could do it, and so, they headed for the flanks of the mountain as quickly as they could. Little did they know that a century after they scaled its height, the mountain would erupt in a shower of ash and lava that would bury multiple towns and kill thousands of people. Their new hiding place was none other than Mount Vesuvius.

Spartacus and his comrades may not have known that they were climbing to the peak of an active volcano, but even if they did, perhaps they would have counted it less of a risk than staying in that awful gladiator school where they all had been slowly losing their minds.

One can imagine the thrill that Spartacus felt as he and his gladiators bolted toward the towering peak. Fear nipped at his heels, driving him faster as the threat of pursuing guards chased him on, but there was something else that was exhilarating, too—something as pure and wild as the mountain wind that filled his lungs. It was freedom. He knew then, whether he lived or died or made it to the peak or not, that he would be doing it as a free man.

But he didn't die on the flank of that volcano. Instead, Spartacus, Crixus, Oenomaus, and their comrades (it is uncertain how many of the original 78 survived the flight from Capua) made it. Despite a brief battle with the pursuing guards, they made it all the way up to the sheltering peak of Mount Vesuvius, where Batiatus and his guards would have difficulty tracking them. In fact, for a moment, it felt as though they had made it to safety, but Spartacus knew better than to let his guard down.

Their escape had only just begun. Spartacus knew that the Romans would be coming, and the same law that had been true in the arena would be true now.

Fight or die.

Chapter 5 – Ambush

With the trek to Mount Vesuvius improbably, and yet undeniably, having succeeded, Spartacus and his comrades dug in and started to prepare for the future. Whether they'd expected to get this far or not, they were quickly able to formulate a plan.

While the idea of slaves escaping and rebelling against their erstwhile masters may be heady stuff in a world where slavery has largely been abolished, there's nothing to indicate that abolition was ever on Spartacus' radar. His goal was much simpler. All he wanted to do was escape. But considering that he came from the center of the world's greatest empire at the time, escape was not a simple thing. He would have to cover thousands of miles, miles that were swarming with Roman soldiers, in order to get away from Roman captivity once and for all. And all of his comrades were coming with him.

By the time they had reached Mount Vesuvius, Spartacus, Crixus, and Oenomaus had seen to it that they would be relatively well provided for. The journey from Capua to the mountain had taken them through fertile farmland, and the men and women that were tending those fields were sitting ducks to a group of gladiators. Spartacus led his band of liberated warriors to raid the farms for food, equipment, and weapons. The success of their raids was variable when it came to much-needed equipment, but at least they could get enough food to sustain themselves for a while, as well as arm themselves more thoroughly. Exchanging kitchen knives for axes, picks, and hoes, Spartacus and his men made it to Vesuvius feeling considerably more confident than when they'd fled the gladiator school.

Finding a hiding place on Mount Vesuvius was hardly difficult. Now a barren wasteland surrounding a smoking crater, Vesuvius was once a green and fertile place, covered with foliage and vines. It was difficult to traverse, too; three sides of the mountain were rocky cliffs that dropped off hundreds of feet to certain death. There was only one way up, and Spartacus' men, once they reached the peak, carefully watched it. The gladiators holed up in the thick cover, and after some time, they realized that no one had found them. A collective sigh of relief ran through the hasty camp, and the escapees began to ask themselves a new question: now what?

The person with the answer to that question seemed to be Spartacus. He had plenty of military experience under his belt, and besides, there was something about the fire in him that lit a spark in the others. They elected him as their leader, and Crixus and Oenomaus were both seconds-in-command. There may also have been lesser-ranking commanders in the group.

Oenomaus and Crixus were both powerful gladiators in their own right, but no one could match Crixus for sheer pig-headed determination. The curly-headed gladiator had endured much in his life, and there was a bitterness in his heart that longed for more than escape. He wanted vengeance. In those early days, Spartacus managed to convince Crixus that escape was their primary goal, but there was a tension already present between the Thracian and the Gaul. The cheers of the Roman public had gone to Crixus' head. He held onto his pride to ward off his fear, forgetting that the very same people who cheered for his victory would have cheered equally for his grisly demise and defeat.

It wasn't long after the gladiator leaders had been elected that their leadership was put to the test. Bitterly complaining about the loss of his valuable gladiators, Batiatus had reported the incident to Rome, demanding that a legion come and recapture his warlike prisoners since it was certainly too great a task for him and his guards. Rome's response was not what Batiatus had hoped. And part of this was because the Roman legions were not near Rome.

The First Mithridatic War, which had kept Sulla so busy in Pontus, eventually erupted into two more wars. The Third Mithridatic War, which started in 75 BCE and wouldn't end until 63 BCE, was a large enough threat that many of the Roman legions were occupied with fighting in it. And in Spain, Quintus Sertorius, a former Marian commander, had stirred up a revolt that was almost on the same scale as Sulla's civil wars. The Roman Republic was in its death throes, and its greatness would only be reborn as the Roman Empire in several decades' time. For now, though, its legions were much too busy trying to uphold its crumbling borders to deal with a bunch of escapees.

Something did have to be done, however, and that was where Gaius Claudius Glaber came in. Glaber was a praetor, which was a high-ranking Roman official. He was told to sort out the gladiator problem so that Rome's higher ranks could continue to focus on more important matters.

Little is known about Glaber except for his involvement with fighting Spartacus. However, from his actions at Vesuvius, one can venture to deduce that his laziness was matched only by his arrogance.

In the absence of the rigorously trained legionaries, Glaber had to seek manpower elsewhere, and so, he raised an ad hoc militia on the spur of the moment. His men were recruited from the surrounding area and were largely untrained; given some armor, weapons, and pay, they were told all they had to do was capture a handful of escaped slaves. Easy, right? Recruitment wasn't hard, and

Glaber didn't anticipate any part of his task as being hard at all. He believed that a bunch of dumb slaves couldn't possibly hope to stand against a Roman militia, even if it didn't consist of legionaries.

There were several factors that Glaber hadn't considered, however. The first was that Spartacus' group no longer consisted of just 78 gladiators. The landscape through which the gladiators had fled, the farms they had raided, and even the fertile flanks of the mountain were all thickly populated with slaves. Herdsmen tending their master's flocks, hapless workers tilling in the fields, even girls working in the homes of farmers—these men and women didn't swing swords or train hard as the gladiators had. In fact, they couldn't have looked more different from the muscular gladiators if they'd tried. But gladiator or no, all these Roman slaves shared one thing in common: they wanted to be free. And Spartacus, somehow, had done it. He'd broken his shackles and fled to the mountainside, and the slaves of the surrounding area followed him in droves.

By the time Glaber sought to attack and recapture Spartacus and his men, the Thracian's group numbered in the thousands, although the exact number is unknown. Glaber's 3,000 men, which was thought to be overly sufficient faced with less than a hundred escapees, would not be as adequate as he had originally thought.

The other factor Glaber hadn't thought of was that Spartacus and many of his comrades were far more than ordinary slaves. They were gladiators, and some of them saw actual battle more frequently than a Roman legionary. These men fought for their lives day in and day out, and it was all they trained for. It was all they *were*, in the eyes of their masters. What was more, Spartacus had been a Roman soldier long before he became a gladiator, and he understood how Romans commanded their troops. He knew his enemy with a bitter intimacy.

Totally failing to account for Spartacus' prowess, Glaber gathered up his band of impromptu soldiers and marched on Vesuvius. Looking at the mountain, he decided that capturing the slaves would be childishly simple. Vesuvius provided plenty of cover, but there was little in the way of provisions to be scavenged from it. Cut them off from the farmlands, Glaber reasoned, and they'd have no choice but to come down. He wouldn't even have to fight them. Starvation would be his only weapon: they would either come down from the mountain or starve up there, and either way worked for him.

Besieging Mount Vesuvius wouldn't be difficult, either, with its single route up and down from the peak. Glaber brought his army over to the only way up the mountain and plopped them down for a leisurely siege that shouldn't make anyone break a sweat. In fact, he seems to have failed to send scouts out or even arrange sentries among his ranks. They just kicked back their heels and relaxed, waiting for a few half-starved and desperate slaves to come stumbling out of the bushes toward them.

They didn't expect a group of warriors to appear out of the cliffs themselves and attack.

Spartacus knew that, large though his force may now be, attacking the Romans head-on would be a death sentence. Instead, he decided to do what Roman commanders often failed to account for—he thought outside the box. Glaber would be expecting Spartacus and his men to come straight down the mountain toward them on the one route that could be taken on foot. So, Spartacus' men would do the opposite.

They would come down the cliffs.

The men and women in the camp set to work. Gathering some of the many green vines that grew all over the mountain, they braided them together, forming springy green ropes that could hold the weight of a powerful gladiator. Once the ropes were done and night had fallen, Spartacus and the bravest of his men headed for the clifftops. Quietly, they secured the ropes at the top of the cliffs, gripped their weapons, and rappelled down the steep and rocky slopes to land feet first in the middle of the Roman camp.

Utter chaos broke loose. Torches were knocked over, and screams echoed through the night, as sleeping soldiers found themselves faced with desperate bare-chested gladiators wielding biting axes and razor-sharp cleavers. Terror reigned in the camp as the disorganized militia abruptly decided that no matter how much Glaber was paying them, it wasn't enough to fight these men who'd appeared from nowhere. They scattered, being cut down where they fled. Glaber is not mentioned in any historical account following the Battle of Mount Vesuvius, and while he may simply have retired and faded into obscurity after this embarrassment, it's entirely possible that he was one of the many who fell that day in the face of the gladiators.

The Romans were utterly routed. They fled back down the mountain, abandoning their camp just as it was. To Spartacus and his followers, the emptied camp was a boon, giving them an abundance of armor, weapons, and horses. They were able to hold real weapons again at last. There was also the presence of something that many of the slaves hadn't possessed in a long time, if they'd ever even had it before: money. To people whose right to own anything had long since been ripped away, the sight of gold and silver coins must have been quite intoxicating. Spartacus made himself even more popular when he decided that the entire bounty of their spoils would be fairly and equally divided among all the slaves, even though he could have easily kept it all for himself.

One can only imagine the scale of the jubilation in that destroyed Roman camp that night. Perhaps they found some wine among the Roman belongings. Maybe there was dancing, and perhaps even a little music, knowing that they had just accomplished the impossible. They had money and security now. They had a leader they trusted.

But that leader, as he gathered together the weapons and armor, knew that their fight was far from over. Their initial escape may have ended, but the war was just beginning.

The Third Servile War was born beneath the cliffs that night. And the scale of its devastation and destruction had never been seen in a slave uprising before.

Chapter 6 – Facing the Legions

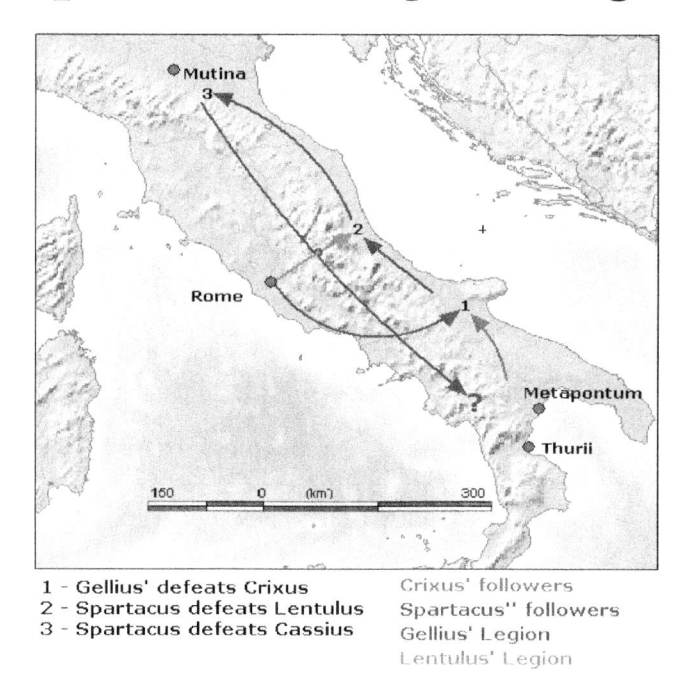

1 - Gellius' defeats Crixus
2 - Spartacus defeats Lentulus
3 - Spartacus defeats Cassius

Crixus' followers
Spartacus'' followers
Gellius' Legion
Lentulus' Legion

Illustration II: A map of events according to Plutarch

Glaber's defeat by Spartacus and the rest of the slaves did not strike the Romans as a threat. Instead, it was something potentially even worse to a culture that prided itself on being superior on every level, including the divine one: it was an insult. A hideous insult to the prowess of Rome. The fact that a bunch of lowly slaves was able to best a praetor was as good as if Spartacus himself had walked up to a consul and spat in his eye.

Rome was determined to sweep Spartacus and the defeat of Glaber under the rug as quickly as possible. Even though the legions were otherwise occupied, the leadership of Rome decided that the best way to get rid of this pesky band of escaped slaves would be to send a couple of the legions to wipe them out once and for all. Another praetor was elected for the role of defeating Spartacus: Publius Varinius.

Varinius was a more cautious man than Glaber. Given the command of several thousand legionaries—likely around 6,000—he decided that facing Spartacus would take some real thinking, not simply barging around as Glaber had done. He was also aware that Spartacus' ranks had swollen vastly from the 78 men who'd escaped Capua, as there had been several thousand at the Battle of Mount Vesuvius. Varinius could never have anticipated exactly how many slaves had joined Spartacus' movement, however. The truth was that there were already about 40,000 men fighting on Spartacus' side.

One move of Spartacus', however, was working to Varinius' advantage. Growing in numbers, the slaves were getting bolder. They were also running out of provisions. Mount Vesuvius had been a good hiding place for a hundred men; forty thousand men were beginning to stretch its resources very thin. Spartacus was being forced to send raiding parties farther and farther afield in a bid to feed his growing army.

Varinius knew that it wouldn't be necessary for him to scale Vesuvius. He could attack Spartacus out in the open country now, and that was exactly what he intended to do. Dividing the bulk of his army up into two groups, he sent them out in a pincer attack, attempting to crush Spartacus' army between the long arms of his own. The first group, commanded by Lucius Furius, consisted of

2,000 men. The rest of the army was split between Lucius Cossinius and a small vanguard with Varinius.

Furius and his men reached the slaves first, unfortunately for them. A group of slaves, possibly commanded by Crixus, lay in wait for the Romans and launched a devastating surprise attack. Furius' column was utterly destroyed, his men routed, and the commander himself killed in the battle. Spartacus himself had gone hunting for Cossinius; the Roman commander may not have expected the slaves to actively seek him out, but they did. Around six miles from Vesuvius, Spartacus found Cossinius preparing for a battle at Herculaneum. He attacked, decimated Cossinius' legions, and set Cossinius himself to flight. Spartacus turned to search for Varinius next, but some of the slaves broke off from the main army and pursued Cossinius as he fled. They caught up to him in the end and butchered him, just like thousands of them had been butchered for the entertainment of his people.

The remnants of the Roman legions regrouped with Varinius, tattered, shocked, and battle-weary from fighting the slaves. As for Spartacus, he realized now that he didn't need Vesuvius anymore. He'd just beaten the Roman legions themselves in open battle, and his own forces were tremendously large, larger than the legions could hope to send against him thanks to their involvement in distant wars. Spartacus realized that he could go wherever he wanted. And where he wanted to be was as far as possible from Rome.

He swung his slaves to the south, hoping to find a route to freedom, and marched away from the home of their oppressors. Crixus was dismayed. The brotherly affection between him and Spartacus erupted, as it often did, into heavy arguing. Victory against the legions had gone to Crixus' head; he believed that they could achieve more. That they could damage Rome as sorely as it had damaged them, and that they could take from Rome what it loved as surely as it had taken away their freedom. Anger and bitterness had been building for so long in Crixus' heart, fueled by every fight in the gladiatorial arena, that he wanted nothing more than to satiate his lust for vengeance. But Spartacus held firm. He wanted to set these people free, not lead them into battle. So, they journeyed south, and Varinius, replenishing his numbers, followed warily behind.

The Roman finally was able to pitch his battle against Spartacus when they'd reached the distant southern town of Lucania. Here, Varinius ran into trouble before he even saw Spartacus and the slaves. Winter was approaching, and the morale among his troops was at a desperate low as they faced the dropping temperatures. What was more, rumors had been circulating through the camp that Spartacus was dividing the spoils equally among his men. Varinius certainly didn't do the same, and some of the lower-ranking soldiers were beginning to wonder if they were fighting on the right side of this war. By now, Spartacus' army did not consist solely of escaped slaves. There were freedmen there now, fighting for a better life, as they knew that the Roman Republic was crumbling around them and hoped that Spartacus would be able to lead them to something better. None of Spartacus' men were slaves anymore: they were rebels.

As a result, Varinius' men began to refuse to fight at all. While he could punish them harshly for desertion and for disobeying his orders, Varinius couldn't physically force them to fight, and so it was with a reduced army and rock-bottom morale that the praetor turned to meet Spartacus at Lucania.

Varinius came perilously close to sharing the fate of his commanders. His unhappy troops clashed miserably with Spartacus' fired-up warriors in a battle that rapidly turned into a humiliating rout. Despite Varinius' more careful tactics, his men were put to flight as surely as Glaber's had been. In fact, the praetor himself was almost captured and/or killed. Rebels seized him, pulling him from his horse. Somehow—likely thanks to a rally of his troops—Varinius was saved, but the rebels returned triumphantly to their camp, leading the praetor's horse between them. The majestic animal was a symbol to them of how close they'd come to taking down a praetor when, only months before, their backs had been covered in scars from the lashes of mere farmers and miners.

Having defeated every adversary that had been set before him, Spartacus entered the winter of 73 BCE feeling confident that he would finally be able to achieve what classical historians presume was his end goal: going home. His army was tens of thousands strong, and it would continue to grow to a force that eventually numbered as many as 120,000. Crixus was urging him to march on Rome itself, to take down the city and rebuild a better world. Dizzy with the scent of victory, many of Spartacus' men would have followed him if he had chosen to lay siege to the capital of the world. But Spartacus had tasted victory many times before—serving in the legions, fighting in the gladiatorial arena, and now as a rebel leader. Victory was good, but home was better.

Still, he was aware that moving 120,000 rebels out of the Roman Republic was no mean feat, and there would be battles to fight along the way. That winter, the Romans left Spartacus largely alone, and he and his men dug in and trained hard as the days grew shorter and the nights colder. Spartacus drove his men hard, encouraging him with his charismatic leadership, as he knew that their victories were nothing compared to what was still to come. They may have beaten some legions, but those legions hadn't been the experienced, battle-hardened men who'd just come home from Spain and Pontus. Those were war veterans fresh off the front, and this time, Spartacus knew, they wouldn't underestimate the rebels.

When spring brought its warm green blush to the Italian countryside, the rift between Spartacus and Crixus grew even wider. Spartacus wanted to take the army straight toward Gaul, seeking the easiest and quickest route out of Roman territory. He wanted to go home, and he wanted to send the slaves home, or at least into freedom. But Crixus had been living off the spoils of his raiding and plundering for too long. He liked fighting. He liked winning more than just the cheers of a jabbering crowd. He liked his growing wealth. And perhaps he believed that the rebels could overthrow Rome itself.

Spartacus and Crixus could not agree, but Spartacus wouldn't force his friend—a man who had become like a brother to him, if a somewhat quarrelsome one—to obey him. Besides, many of the rebels wanted to follow Crixus and continue the war. So, Spartacus split the army in two. He and those who wanted to escape the Roman Republic turned toward Gaul; Crixus and his fellow raiders, numbering around 30,000, went south, heading deep into Italy where the farmlands were waiting to be plundered.

It was a terrible mistake.

Rome had finally awoken to the real danger posed by the rebels. Clearly, this was a problem beyond the praetors; it would take real legions, battle-seasoned and commanded by men of the highest rank, to put a stop to the chaos that Spartacus and Crixus were sowing all over the Republic. Multiple Roman legions were sent out, and these were commanded by the consuls. One was Gnaeus Cornelius Lentulus Clodianus, and the other was Lucius Gellius Publicola.

Publicola struck first. Discovering Crixus' smaller force under the shadows of Mount Gargano, where they were raiding Roman towns with merry abandon, the consul decided that it was time to teach these arrogant rebels a lesson. He attacked.

Crixus may have done well to flee, to find a defensible position, or to seek reinforcements from Spartacus. Yet at his heart, Crixus was a gladiator, not a commander. He only knew one way to respond to a threat: to attack. Seeing the legions rush down upon him, Crixus knew no fear. He ordered his men forward, and he rushed into the battle with the kind of courage that had kept him alive in the arena.

It did not serve him so well here, not when there were tens of thousands of soldiers involved, and not when he should have been working on strategies instead of charging blindly into battle. Thirty thousand rebels started the battle with Publicola on that bloody day in the spring of 72 BCE; only ten thousand were left when the fight was over. And Crixus was not one of them. It was a hopeless, humiliating defeat, and it was the last battle Crixus would ever fight.

When the news reached Spartacus, it broke his heart. As much as Crixus had argued with him, as warlike and arrogant as the Gaul had been, they had been friends in the worst of circumstances. The darkness and the chains back in Capua had bonded them as brothers. And now dear, stupid, proud, stubborn, brave Crixus was dead.

Spartacus' grief turned dark and bitter in his heart. He remembered the glorious funerals that the Romans had always held to honor the dead; he remembered, also, having to fight to commemorate dead Romans. He remembered the roots of the gladiatorial games, and a dark idea formed in his mind. Something about the death of Crixus snapped something deep inside Spartacus. He wanted to do to the Romans what they had done to him, to Crixus, and to the others.

It is presumed that the body of the dead rebel general was never recovered, but Spartacus was determined to give him a funeral anyway, a funeral worthy of a general and not a mere gladiator. Gladiators died in the public eye and were buried in ignominy, but Crixus was going to be given the send-off of a high-ranking Roman official. And that meant that Spartacus would need to throw gladiatorial games of his own to honor the dead.

It was a bitterly twisted day when the black smoke of Crixus' empty pyre rose up against the Italian sun and Spartacus watched as his gladiators lined up to face each other. Only these gladiators weren't slaves and foreigners. They were prisoners of war. They were Romans. Spartacus watched with satisfaction as he saw these well-trained warriors forget their honor, their glory, and their social standing. He watched the look in their eyes change from triumph to fear. He watched them fight the way he had once fought: desperately, in terror, for their lives.

Fight or die.

Chapter 7 – The Lone Volunteer

When the Roman prisoners all lay dead around the camp, and Spartacus was satisfied that Crixus had been thoroughly honored, he turned his attention to vengeance. The army that had killed his friend and destroyed a large portion of his army was still out there, and they were rapidly maneuvering to do to Spartacus what they had done to Crixus. Clodianus was heading as fast as his men could march for the Alps, hoping to corner Spartacus before he could escape the Republic, while Publicola was stalking him from behind. Their hope was to crush Spartacus and the rebels between the two of them and put a stop to the rebellion once and for all. They were expecting Spartacus to keep fleeing toward the Alps, toward home.

Home was where Spartacus was going, but he was by no means going to flee the consuls. He was ready to attack now. Even though the legions were better armed than his rebels, Spartacus had an ace up his sleeve: a strong cavalry regiment. They had been unable to procure horses when they had first escaped from Capua, but Spartacus and many of the rebels were Thracian, and they'd been taming the wild horses that roamed the mountainsides of Thrace for generations. Capturing wild horses or stealing farm horses and turning them into reliable cavalry mounts was child's play for these men.

One would like to imagine that Spartacus had kept Varinius' horse for himself, a strong, beautiful animal that had once borne a Roman praetor and now carried the gladiator who had defeated him. Either way, Spartacus had a cavalry, and he put it to good use. Clodianus was still waiting for the approach of a lumbering band of infantry when Spartacus and his cavalry burst out of the landscape and swooped down upon the legions. Caught by surprise, Clodianus and his men didn't have the time to rally. Spartacus' cavalry cut straight through Clodianus' legions, and the consul was sent back to Rome with his tail between his legs, his army routed, and all of his supplies stolen by the rebels.

Punching right through the consuls' trap, Spartacus continued toward the Alps as the winter of 72 BCE settled cold and dark on the landscape. Clodianus and Publicola, thoroughly beaten, had to return to Rome in ignominy. The leaders of Rome—the two single men wielding the most power in the whole Roman Republic—had let it down. The rebels were still on the loose, and their force was still growing. The Senate, however, decided that its consuls were clearly unfit to lead the army. They perhaps also thought that the risk of both of them getting killed in a battle would cause too much instability and panic in Rome; already, the Romans were terrified that Spartacus was going to wheel around and attack the great city itself.

Another leader would have to be found, one who would willingly face the rebels and seek a resounding and lasting victory. The Senate began to ask for volunteers among the patriarchy. Most men backed away, knowing that being beaten by the rebels was political suicide.

Most men. One—and one alone—volunteered to go and meet Spartacus on the battlefield. And that man was Marcus Licinius Crassus.

Crassus had been rolling in money for years. His wily real estate schemes and smooth-talking politics had won him both wealth and power, and his reputation for being a generous host had also gifted him with popularity. That Spanish cave overlooking the sea must have seemed like it was ages ago, and yet Crassus, for all his wealth, could still not satiate a furious hunger that burned inside him. That hunger was envy, and that envy was of Pompey. The young general had amassed glory upon glory in his battles in the Mithridatic Wars, Sulla's civil wars, and now in the Sertorian War in Spain. Sulla had even bestowed upon Pompey the highest possible honor for a military man: a triumph, or a long, glamorous parade through the streets of Rome. Crassus wanted a triumph, too. He wanted to be as glorious in the eyes of the people as Pompey. He wanted to play second fiddle to no one.

To Crassus' delight, Pompey was thoroughly out of the way when the call came for volunteers to go up against Spartacus. Sertorius' revolt in Spain was still in full force, and so, Pompey's hands were full with fighting in the land where Crassus had once hidden in a dark cave. This was Crassus' chance to shine. He jumped at the opportunity, and since he was the only man who volunteered to fight Spartacus, he was immediately given the job and the full command of the legions in Italy.

Morale among those legions had been low throughout the rebellion, and they had never been lower than they were at that moment. Many remembered how others had refused to fight Spartacus at all back when they were under Varinius' command; perhaps those who refused had chosen wisely, considering the utter defeat that the legions had suffered at Lucania. Others had tasted briefly of victory against Crixus only to see Spartacus slip out of their fingers once again. Perhaps they were tired of the surprises that Spartacus was continually throwing at them—abseiling down cliff walls on vines or mustering a whole cavalry regiment out of nowhere. They never knew what this Thracian was going to do next.

Another factor that must have had an effect on Roman morale was the fact that the war was being fought in Italy, which was the homeland of many of these legionaries. They would have seen acres of farmland, villages, and towns that looked like the places where they'd grown up. They would have also seen them all razed to the ground, trampled into blood and dirt, and raided bare. Spartacus was a hero to the rebels, but to the legions, he was a terrifying threat. What was more, he was inspiring thousands of slaves to leave their posts and follow him. The implication for the Roman economy was great, but greater still was the fear that free Romans had of their own slaves now. They were aware that there were more slaves than free people living in the Roman Republic. If all the slaves revolted, it could spell death and disaster.

Thus, it was a very disheartened army that Crassus found at his disposal, one that was sick of the humiliation of being defeated by a mere gladiator. Crassus was good with words, but it would take more than smooth-talking to inspire this disheartened bunch—and before going up against Spartacus, Crassus knew that he would have to whip this sorry band of miserable legionaries into shape. Perhaps he could have done this with inspiration or the promise of great rewards. Instead, Crassus wielded the greatest weapon of all against his own men: fear.

The word "decimation" today is defined as large-scale killing or destruction. In ancient Rome, it had a much more specific meaning, coming from the Latin root of "decem," or "ten." Yet even then, the word was ominous, and it was guaranteed to strike terror into the heart of any Roman soldier. Decimation was a thing to be horribly feared, and with good reason, as it meant the killing of one-tenth of a Roman legion as punishment for poor performance in battle.

Even in the 1st century BCE, decimation was already an ancient punishment, and it had only been rarely used even when it was fairly popular around the 5th century BCE. In fact, it hadn't been used for decades when Crassus strutted into his command of the legions, but that didn't stop him from inflicting it upon his men. As soon as the announcement was made, a hush of silent terror fell upon the Roman camp. Every soldier knew that he might not see the end of the day.

One by one, lots were cast for each of the legions that Crassus wanted to punish for their inability to stop Spartacus. It was a deadly gamble, a game of human lives. Out of every ten soldiers, one would have to die. And once that man was chosen, the nine comrades who lived were forced to take up heavy cudgels and bludgeon their brother-in-arms to death. These men had fought together, lived together, and were ready to die together on the battlefield. Instead, they had to kill each other, brutally and violently, bones crunching under the savage blows of the clubs, and the blood of friends splattering hot and salty on their faces.

When it was done, Crassus' army was one-tenth smaller than it had been before his decimation. The men who remained were given only raw barley to eat that night, and they ate it slowly, their fear making the bitter grain turn to sawdust on their tongues. They knew one thing for sure: angering Crassus would be a terrible mistake.

There was no adversary that could frighten them as much as Crassus just did. And so, these men would fight to the death for him, their lives suddenly governed by the same rule that had driven Spartacus from one victory to the next in the gladiatorial games. Now, fight or die had become the reality for Romans who considered themselves to be free.

Chapter 8 – At the Feet of the Alps

Illustration III: It's easy to see why the Italian Alps appeared so forbidding to Spartacus' men

The terrified troops that now found themselves under the command of Crassus might have expected to be marched immediately to the north. But Crassus, heartless though he may have been, was also a wily commander. He knew that simply punishing his men and sending them back into battle wasn't going to be an effective strategy. Instead, he began to train them, working through the winter by taking money out of his own pocket to equip and train the eight legions he'd been given, which was around 40,000 men, to the best of his ability. This was not simply about winning a war or defending his country from a rebellion. To Crassus, this was personal. It didn't even matter that Crassus had never laid eyes on Spartacus before—the Thracian now represented to Crassus the only obstacle lying between him and equal greatness to Pompey. Envy proved to be a powerful motivator.

Meanwhile, Spartacus continued to push north as fast as his men could march, but there was one more mighty obstacle lying between them and the Alps: Mutina, which was commanded by Gaius Cassius Longinus Varus. Now called Modena, this city was where Longinus ruled over Cisalpine Gaul as its governor, and it was the last great obstacle between Spartacus and the Alps. The gladiator general knew that if he could reach the Alps and cross them, he'd be almost home free. No Roman legion would pursue him over those great mountains.

But Spartacus also had to hurry. Winter was coming; 72 BCE was drawing to a close, and he needed to get his men over those mountains before the snow made them utterly impassable. If that took him through Mutina, then so be it, no matter who was standing in his way.

Longinus' son, who shared the same name as his father but is better known as Cassius, would later become legendary for his involvement in the assassination of Julius Caesar. But all that was almost thirty years in the future, and right now, Longinus was just a governor bent on protecting his piece of the Roman Republic from the marauding army of the gladiators—and they were indeed marauding. Spartacus now had more than 100,000 followers, and all those men and women had to be fed somehow. They had been plundering ever since they left Capua, and those raids were now occurring on a grand scale. While the defeat of the legions had left them with plenty of armor and weapons, provisions still needed to be scrounged from the farmlands. The slaves that continued to escape and join the rebellion had little regard for the lives of those who had oppressed them. Civilians were killed, crops destroyed, and livestock was slaughtered and carried off to feed the insatiable army.

The raiding was made worse by the fact that Spartacus was pushing as fast as he could, refusing to stop or slow down for anything, not even to carry provisions with him. He slaughtered the pack animals for food and burned all the supplies that couldn't be easily carried. Ruthlessly pushing his army—which by now included children and the elderly, as slaves brought their families with them, hoping to take them to freedom—Spartacus reached Mutina before winter came.

Here, once again, a Roman army stood between him and his homeland, and once again, Spartacus and his men rallied to defeat it. Longinus didn't stand a chance. The provincial army was thoroughly defeated at Mutina, and the way was thrown wide open for Spartacus to take his gigantic army to the Alps and cross over into Thrace.

Spartacus was almost home. But he didn't go. Instead, his entire enormous contingent, exhausted from weeks of hard marching, came shuddering to a halt at the feet of the mighty Alps.

With the nip of winter in the air, the plain where Spartacus made his camp was richly painted in reds and browns, the glowing colors of fall still all around them. It looked warm and inviting; the crops were still ripe in the fields that his people were plundering. There were cooking fires and the smell of wood smoke and children laughing down here on the plain. But ahead of them, the Alps rose like a tremendous rampart, a monumental rock wall stabbing up into the sky, already streaked with snow. There were no gentle rises, no apparent pass, and no visible way to cross those great mountains. Spartacus knew it could be done, but it didn't look that way. The mountains were more than daunting. They looked impassable.

He hadn't come all this way just to give up because of the mountains he'd always known he had to climb, though. It had seemed an easier task when there had just been 78 strong and fit gladiators to get to the other side. Even with tens of thousands of followers, Spartacus seemed to have wanted to try. But something stopped him on that plain in the fall of 72 BCE, at the very feet of the last obstacle standing between him and the homeland he was yearning for. No one really knows why. It's possible that his vast following was simply too daunted by the great peaks. Perhaps, news of Thrace had reached them, too. All was not well in the homeland that Spartacus wanted to return to.

Even though Thrace had, for many years, been more or less under Roman control, it was not a province of the Roman Republic, not when Spartacus had walked those heady mountainsides, anyway. It was a client kingdom: meekly submissive to Rome and obliged to provide the great Republic with some of its resources but still able to govern itself as it pleased. Except the winds of change were blowing across Spartacus' ancestral highlands, and they didn't smell good. Rumors were reaching him that Rome had actually appointed the new king. That made Thrace little more than a Roman province—and it meant that the Thracian king was a Roman ally. How could Spartacus return to a country governed by his enemies? If Rome found out that Spartacus and the other escaped slaves were in Thrace, the new king would easily hand them over. And then it would have been better if they'd simply stayed put and remained slaves for the rest of their lives.

To make matters worse, Crixus' ambitions had infected many of the rebels. Defeating a Roman consul, then a governor, — was a mighty and incredible feat, and it went to their heads. Spartacus' tantalizing offer of returning back home had lost its savor in the face of victory upon victory. What was home in comparison with continuing to plunder these rich fields? There were whispers among the rebels of marching on Rome itself, taking down the city, and building something better. The sweet sound of liberty had been drowned out in the crescendo of power.

We can only speculate on which of these factors—or, perhaps, which combination of these factors—caused Spartacus to do what he did next. Almost within sight of Thrace, the Thracian turned around. He headed back down from the Alps and began to move toward the south of Italy, his men free once more to plunder as they pleased. Not all of them chose to continue raiding Italy, however. Spartacus allowed his followers to choose whether they wanted to risk crossing the frigid Alps for the promise of going home or to stay with the main army and attempt to conquer more of the Roman Republic. Ten thousand men wisely chose to go back to their homelands. As Plutarch did, we could assume that Spartacus' heart went with them, but he felt a duty to remain as the military leader of the men who refused to cross the Alps.

For a time, the fortune and skill that had so favored Spartacus since his rebellion began continued to pursue them as they moved toward the southernmost tip of Italy. Crassus was training his troops, biding his time, and so, Spartacus was largely unopposed except by local garrisons as he and his men swept ever southward. They moved fast, too; fast enough that many in Rome were terrified that the time had come at last that their slaves would overthrow them. Spartacus knew better than to attempt to attack the great city itself, however. This may have been the plan eventually, but he had to build up their strength, equipment, and numbers first. Instead, he kept going past Rome and pushed toward the sea.

Sometime in the winter of 72/71 BCE, they arrived at the southwestern tip of Italy, a province then known as Bruttium, where he and his men were using their plunder to their advantage. The supplies they didn't need were traded (many merchants didn't seem to care who they dealt with, Roman or rebel, as long as they were paid) for metals with which to manufacture more armor and weaponry. Spartacus' army was made up of ex-slaves, after all. They knew how to work with their hands.

Perhaps in preparation for fighting a bigger city, Spartacus set his sights on the town of Thurii. The ancient town, whose foundations were laid in the mid-5th century BCE, was subjected to a swift and efficient attack from Spartacus and his men. It appears as though it may have surrendered quickly and willingly; there was no damage to the city, and there does not appear to have been many casualties according to historical records, although Spartacus did compel the citizens to pay him a heavy tribute, not to mention his men who helped themselves to supplies. It was the first time that the rebels had taken a town.

It was also one of their last great victories. Crassus had patiently watched and waited as the rebels dug in and spent the winter happily in Thurii. His men had been training hard, driven by the terror of their leader. He knew that if he was going to stop Spartacus, he wouldn't have much time—at least, not if he was going to do it personally. Rumor had it that Pompey's attempts to put down the revolt in Spain were growing more and more successful. Soon, he would win, and he would come back to Rome, and he would take over from Crassus, and there would be no glory for the jealous praetor.

Envy in the north. Greed in the south. There would-be no-good end to this tale.

Chapter 9 – Defeat

When spring came again in 71 BCE, both Crassus and Spartacus were on the move.

Spartacus' goal at this point in time is uncertain, although he may well have been trying to march on Rome; his men left Thurii and headed northward, their ranks swollen with numbers, steel weapons gleaming in the hands of each rebel soldier. Three long years of war had beaten Spartacus' army from a rag-tag bunch of escaped slaves into a real military force, good enough to beat even Rome's best. Now, he moved them toward Lucania, where they had fought that glorious victory against Varinius in the very first year of the war. Perhaps the soil upon which so much Roman blood had been spilled would prove to be a good battleground once more.

Crassus' goal, on the other hand, is abundantly clear. He wanted to stop Spartacus, and he wanted to do it as quickly and gloriously as possible. As his practice of decimation had proven, Crassus wouldn't let mere ethics or moral issues stand in his way. He wanted victory, he wanted it fast, and he wanted it at all costs.

When Spartacus' army began to move, Crassus moved just as quickly. He arrayed six of his eight legions along the borders of Picenum, near Picentia, and remained in command of them. The other two legions were entrusted to Crassus' legate, a man named Mummius. Some sources say that these were the very same legions that had once been commanded by the two consuls, the legions that had let Rome down once before. And they were about to do it again.

Spartacus and his men continued to journey north, possibly to Rome or maybe back to the Alps. Perhaps Spartacus had finally managed to convince his wayward army that going home was better than any amount of glory. Or maybe he, too, now believed that Rome was theirs for the taking. Either way, they moved north, just as Crassus had anticipated. Soon, it began to appear to Spartacus that they had no choice except to keep going north. He was likely unaware of Crassus' position at Picentia, but he did know that there was a Roman army following him and that they were very close behind.

Mummius and both his legions had taken a long, circular route around Spartacus' forces. They were now shadowing Spartacus from the south, trying to pressure him into moving more and more northward and straight into the open arms of Crassus and the bulk of the Roman army. Crassus hoped that the sight of two legions—around 10,000 men—would be enough to spook Spartacus into moving faster north. He did give Mummius strict orders, however, not to engage Spartacus under any circumstances. Those same legions had suffered a humiliating defeat under greater commanders than just a legate, as two consuls together hadn't been able to make them beat Spartacus. "Not even a skirmish," Crassus had ordered Mummius sharply.

Unfortunately for Crassus, Spartacus' men knew full well that they'd already fought and beaten two Roman legions, and Mummius' men didn't exactly strike fear into their hearts. If Spartacus' men were aware that Mummius was following them, they appear to have ignored him, waiting for him to make his move.

It seems that Mummius suffered from the same disease as Crassus did: he wanted glory, and he wanted it all to himself. Unlike Crassus, though, Mummius wasn't a cool, calculated military commander who had been hardened by years of tribulation. He thought he knew best, and he also thought he could be the one to beat Spartacus at last. When the opportunity presented itself, Mummius was ready for it. It's uncertain what exactly the circumstances were surrounding the next battle of the Third Servile War; perhaps Spartacus' troops had let their guard down, perhaps they were encamped somewhere indefensible one night, or perhaps Mummius just decided that he could achieve what two consuls hadn't.

Either way, Mummius disobeyed Crassus. He attacked the rebels with his two legions, perhaps hoping for an element of surprise. Surprised though Spartacus might have been, he responded with a violence and a capability that Mummius hadn't been expecting. When the Romans charged, a wall of shining shields coming toward the rebels, the rebels did not flee. Instead, they attacked in a foaming wave of rage, led by the fearsome Spartacus. Their battle cry echoed from one hill to the other, and when they struck, they struck like a thunderbolt. The Roman line could have held, perhaps, if the legionaries had done their duty. But they remembered too well the rout of the previous year when friends and comrades had fallen and died all around them. And when the tidal wave of rebels struck against the standing rocks of the Romans, the line crumbled, not because of casualties but simply because of fear. This means the Roman legionaries did the unthinkable: they fled, throwing down their arms as they went. Even Mummius wheeled his horse around, abandoned his troops, and whipped the beast into the best gallop it could muster, carrying him as swiftly as possible away from the battle.

The fight with Mummius was less a battle than it was a total disgrace. Perhaps somewhat bemused to have so easily beaten yet another set of Roman legions, Spartacus and his men brushed him off as a distraction and kept on moving north while Mummius' legions fled in terror. Perhaps unwisely, they headed back to the main army, where Crassus was surprised to see them. He was even more surprised to see the state that the men were in. When the legionaries had left his army to shadow Spartacus, they had been well-armed. They each had carried a massive wooden shield, a dagger, a meter-long sword called a *spatha*, and a spear. Now, they returned bedraggled and empty-handed, their weapons left behind. Yet there were not many dead or wounded.

Crassus knew from just looking at them that they had seen battle and that they had fled from it. When Mummius arrived and confirmed what Crassus already suspected, he was utterly incensed. Mummius had directly disobeyed Crassus' orders, and the result was a massive drop in morale and the loss of many expensive weapons. Crassus had furnished the army with those weapons out of his own pocket—and what was more, the show of cowardice angered him. Dropping one's weapons in flight was considered to be the height of disgrace all over the ancient world. Crassus wanted this war to glorify him, to make him wonderful, a second Pompey, Crassus Magnus perhaps. Instead, his men had run from the battlefield, and they'd made a fool out of him.

Crassus did not take well to being made a fool of, and he responded with bitter retaliation. Mummius was harshly punished— it is not specified what exactly was done to him, but Crassus may well have punished him physically—and, according to some accounts, this was when the decimation of the two legions took place. Whatever else Crassus did to punish the cowardly legions, he established himself once more in the minds of his army as being far more terrifying than Spartacus. After that, no more legionaries ran away from battle.

The damage, however, was done. Spartacus knew that there were Romans in the area, and he tried to act with more caution. What happened next is a little hazy in the historical accounts. According to Plutarch, he somehow discovered Crassus' army at Picentia without actually engaging them, perhaps by the use of scouts, and then turned back toward Bruttium, knowing that he couldn't beat Crassus. It seems unlikely, however, given that the last time two Roman legions had tried to trap Spartacus between them, he'd simply punched through them and continued on his way.

Appian's account gives a more likely explanation for Spartacus' return toward Bruttium. Spartacus, having encountered the Romans, became cautious. He started to doubt their plan of marching on Rome (if that was the plan at all), advocating instead to move straight back to the Alps and cross over them as they should have done the previous fall. Once again, a group of men refused to listen to him. About 10,000 rebels split off from the main army, following an unnamed leader. It was the last time Spartacus would see them alive.

This new little rebel faction moved closer to Crassus' army, encamping themselves somewhere near him. They did not last long. Crassus discovered them and struck, heavily and savagely, his men driven on with the knowledge that dying in battle was a better alternative to being bludgeoned to death by their own comrades. Several thousand rebels perished, and 900 were taken prisoner. The rest were scattered, their hopes of glory torn apart and thrown to the winds. Some made it back to Spartacus to warn him, but it was already too late. Crassus was coming.

Crassus' troops were now more ready than ever to fight the rebels. They'd had their first taste of victory since the death of Crixus, and they were hungry for more, ready to prove to the Roman Republic that they were still worthy of the title of being the greatest army in the world. None of Spartacus' wily tricks were going to work this time; pitched battle, the type that he had been trying to avoid ever since escaping from Capua, was inevitable. Spartacus would have to fight the Roman legions in the open for the first time, and he knew it could be disastrous.

If he had known just how disastrous it would be, Spartacus might never have even tried to stand against Crassus. The Romans he'd dealt with before had been cowards—Batiatus with his red-hot iron, Varinius abandoning his horse to flee, even Publicola and Clodianus with their inability to get their legions to defeat him. But Crassus was driven by a loathing that devoured any form of fear, and his men fought with the same kind of crazy desperation that Spartacus had known in the gladiatorial arena. When he fought them, he saw something familiar in their eyes—terror. And this time, it wasn't Spartacus that they were afraid of. They fought the way he'd fought other gladiators and wild animals—not because they wanted to fight him but because their own version of Batiatus was waiting for them if they failed to fight well. For the Roman legions, life had been reduced to one brutal fact: fight or die.

The motivator of fear proved to be just as powerful for the legionaries as it had been for the gladiators. Spartacus' rebels were unprepared for the full force of legionaries fighting their hearts out. When they clashed, which probably took place a few weeks after the battle with Mummius, the battle was a disaster, and for the first time, Spartacus himself was forced to retreat. Seeing that the battle was about to turn from mere defeat into annihilation, he took what was left of his men and fled, leaving 6,000 rebels dead on the field.

Spartacus and his men limped back toward Bruttium, shaken by their awful defeat and by the new zest for battle they'd seen in the Romans. For the first time since their revolt, the Romans had fought with a fire that could match that of the slaves. It was the beginning of the end for Spartacus, and he knew it. The fearless faith that his men had had in him was shaken now by defeat, and to make matters worse, Spartacus didn't know how to inspire them anymore. He had been promising them that they could go home.

Now, though, their lust for victory had dragged them back into Italy when they had stood on the very threshold of freedom.

Spartacus' terrible suspicions were coming true. He wasn't going to be able to save them; they should have crossed the Alps when they had reached them in the first place. Now, they were all the way across the country from the Alps, with nowhere to flee except the ocean. Flee they did, however, heading deeper and deeper into the "toe" of Italy, having nowhere else to go. Crassus was hounding them now, engaging them in countless little skirmishes, each one more costly than the last. The rebels began to perish, the army fragmenting, and Spartacus was finally losing control over his massive force. It seemed as though the end was near, as if there was nothing more that Spartacus could do.

But just as Spartacus didn't give up back in the dark cells of Capua, he didn't give up now. Like he had done on the peak of Mount Vesuvius, Spartacus came up with a plan—and this one would be the most unorthodox of them all.

Chapter 10 – Betrayed by the Pirates

The Mediterranean might be the playground of tourists today, but thousands of years ago, it was ruled by pirates.

As early as 1300 BCE, Egyptian pharaohs were writing letters to Far Eastern rulers, telling them about their pirate problem, a problem that was plundering and raiding their shores. This was done by a group known as the Lukka, native to modern-day Turkey. A few hundred years later, in the time of Ramesses the Great (the pharaoh popularly considered to star in the biblical book of Exodus), the fearsome Sea Peoples ravaged the countries along the shore of the Mediterranean, destroying entire cities. Ramesses was the only one who could stop them, which he succeeded in doing around 1178 BCE.

For hundreds of years, the pirates of the Mediterranean continued to harass even the greatest of nations. The slave trade was always the lifeblood of piracy; these seafaring human traffickers would capture people in one country and sell them as slaves to the citizens of another. Ancient Greece fell victim to them with such frequency that a 7th-century hymn describes how a band of pirates, referred to as the Tyrrhenians, captured the Greek god of wine and attempted to sell him into slavery. Dionysus only escaped by turning all of the pirates into dolphins, according to the hymn. Two centuries later, Greece would strike back by fielding some pirates of its own, including a man by the same name as the god of wine, Dionysius the Phocaean, one of the most infamous pirates of all.

These notorious Tyrrhenians may have been Etruscans, the ancient tribe that was, at the same time as the hymns were written, pressuring the citizens of the little town of Rome to form themselves into a kingdom. It would only be in the 3rd century BCE that the Romans themselves, who were now established into the early Roman Republic, would have their first encounter with pirates. Queen Teuta of Illyria (modern-day Balkan Peninsula, including Croatia, Herzegovina, and Bosnia) was following in her late husband's footsteps by attempting to expand her borders. She was one of the first ancient powers to truly invest in piracy as a form of warfare. Her men roamed the Adriatic Sea with instructions to attack and plunder any non-Illyrian vessel that they happened to come across, and so, she created one of the first fleets of buccaneers.

One of Teuta's greatest enemies was the Roman Republic. When Illyrian pirates became a significant problem for Rome, the consul of the time sent out a commander known as Lucius Postumius Albinus, aided by Demetrius of Pharos, to deal with them. Demetrius was an Illyrian and a traitor; his betrayal of Teuta was instrumental in what became known as the First Illyrian War, which lasted from 229 BCE to 228 BCE. Rome won a decisive victory, and the Illyrian pirate problem was solved.

Two hundred years later, Rome still had a pirate problem, except this time, no decisive action would be taken against it. The Tyrrhenians, Illyrians, and Greeks had all been washed away by the tidal wave of time; in their place, the Cilicians had risen up, and these were perhaps the most fearsome of them all.

Cilicia, part of modern-day Turkey, was a relatively new province at the time; Pompey himself would annex it in the 60s BCE. But the pirates that lived there had been terrorizing Rome for much longer than that, and Pompey's conquest of the area would do little to actually stop them. Like the Lukka, who had also inhabited the area, these pirates found it ideal for their illegal operations. The network of coves and little natural bays peppering the shoreline made it easy to conceal ships both from their prey and from those who might try to stop them; there was also an abundance of woods and forests on the shore, making it easy to obtain lumber for building all manner of ships. The pirates themselves were of varying descent, but they all had one thing in common: plunder. The fact that they were not affiliated with any specific country made them more dangerous than any of Teuta's buccaneers. These men were self-serving and wholly independent. They'd cut the throat of any nationality in order to search its pockets.

Like the Tyrrhenians, the Cilician pirates' main focus was on the slave trade, and this was where Rome discovered that these pirates could be useful. Hundreds of thousands of slaves were shipped in from Cilicia to the Roman Republic and sold there; in fact, just as Sicily was Rome's main source of grain, Cilicia became its main source of slaves. This time, there would be no Lucius Postumius Albinus to sally forth and put a stop to slavery. A few half-hearted attempts were made by Marcus Antonius (the grandfather of Mark Antony) to capture Cilicia, but only small portions of the region were ever brought under his control, and even then, the pirates continued with their dastardly work. It was just too convenient to have slaves streaming into the Republic.

The Tyrrhenians might have captured a Greek god, but the Cilicians, in 75 BCE, captured the next best thing: Julius Caesar. Only 25 years old at the time, Caesar was already quick to prove his strategic brilliance, as well as his ruthlessness. The pirates were delighted to have captured a Roman patrician, and instead of selling him into slavery, they decided to post a ransom for him. Caesar was disgusted when he was told that he was being ransomed for only twenty talents of silver. He arrogantly told the pirates that he was worth much more than that, and he bullied them into increasing his ransom to fifty talents of silver.

For the next few weeks, while his associates scrambled to rescue him from the pirate ship, Caesar more or less bossed the pirates around their own ship. He demanded silence while he was sleeping, inserted himself into the pirates' daily activities, and eventually left them with a murderous promise: when his ransom was paid, he was going to have the lot of them crucified. Once freed, Caesar was quick to make good on his promise. He raised a fleet of ships, captured the small island where the pirates were staying, and cut their throats because the proconsul of Asia refused to have them crucified.

The Cilician pirates were about as notorious—both as pirates and as slave traders—as they could be. And to the slaves of Rome, many of whom had passed through their brutal hands and been treated as chattel, they were perhaps even greater enemies than the Romans themselves. That was why it was a tremendous surprise when Spartacus decided to turn to the Cilician pirates for help.

Crassus had been hot on Spartacus' heels ever since their first clash near Picentia. Knowing that he couldn't punch his way through Crassus' army the way he'd done with Publicola and Clodianus, Spartacus continued to move south, and Crassus gleefully pursued, believing that he'd trapped his quarry in Bruttium at last. And it certainly looked that way. Harried by the presence of Crassus, and only a few days ahead of him, Spartacus set up camp at the beginning of 71 BCE on the shores of the Strait of Messina at Rhegium, located at the very southernmost part of Italy. It looked as though he'd been brought to bay, like a treed raccoon with hounds circling the roots.

But Spartacus was not done fighting yet. He had been trapped before, and he had escaped before. The difference was that last time, he had been able to slip away from unwitting guards with the help of 78 others. Now, he had eight Roman legions to face, and he knew that his badly damaged force, which was depleted by the ten thousand who had crossed the Alps and again by the six thousand killed in battle (it's also likely he lost more to disease or cold as well), was not big enough to beat them. He needed reinforcements. And there was only one place left to run to: Sicily.

Sixty years before the time of the Spartacus rebellion, a slave named Eunus had made himself king on the fertile grounds of Sicily, the breadbasket of Italy. The island had always been a place of abundance and agriculture, and where there were farms, there were thousands upon thousands of slaves. Spartacus knew that while he had suffered defeat at the hands of Crassus, he was still a hero in the eyes of the slaves who waited patiently for freedom. If he could make it to Sicily, he would at least have a much more defensible position. He would liberate the slaves there and use them for reinforcements. Even his men would have warm barns to sleep in and more than enough to eat, boosting their morale and their strength. If they could just get to Sicily, they might still have a chance of standing against Crassus.

The only trouble was the Strait of Messina. Nearly three miles wide and eight hundred feet deep, the strait was impassable except by boat. Spartacus had no ships, so there was no way to take tens of thousands of men from the shores of Italy to the abundant fields of Sicily. Taking a military port would be both recklessly ambitious and time-consuming. Roman merchants were steering well clear of the ravaging, ever-hungry rebel army, which had been plundering everywhere it went for years. There was only one option left: the Cilician pirates.

Many of the rebels who now fought in Spartacus' army may have passed through the hands of these cruel human traffickers. Perhaps they remembered swaying in the bellies of those pirate vessels, chained to each other, hopeless in the dark and the sickness and the filth. Once the vessels came ashore, the slaves were dragged out into the sun and stripped naked, then taken to the market with signs hanging around their necks stating their price and other details. They had been poked and prodded by prospective buyers whose eyes ran across their bare bodies with as much respect and dignity as would have been afforded to a piece of furniture. Even a horse was more valuable than most slaves and would have been offered greater care. Then they'd been torn away from the friendships they'd made on those slave ships and sent into new lives, lives of drudgery and abuse, their rights gone, their families forgotten. The Cilician pirates had done this to many of them, and now, Spartacus was turning to them for help. It's likely that the gladiator general faced a fair amount of opposition from his army for this decision, and perhaps rightly so. But Spartacus could see no other way. It was either cross the strait to Sicily on a pirate ship or turn and face the might of eight Roman legions, and he knew that to do so would cause an outright slaughter.

The details have long since been lost to history. Somehow, Spartacus came into contact with a group of the pirates and made a deal with them. Their role was to bring him and all of his men across the strait to Sicily, where, hopefully, their quest for freedom would be renewed. Perhaps Spartacus would even be able to succeed in ruling the island the way Eunus had; it was a poor substitute, in the gladiator's eyes, for going home, but it was better than death. Spartacus had wanted to go back to Thrace, but once again, his hand was being forced by that unrelenting rule that had been presiding over his life ever since he was first captured. *Fight or die.*

We're not sure exactly what Spartacus granted the Cilician pirates in return. He may have offered them a position of power, promising to give them rights to some resources or land in Sicily once he had taken control over the island. It seems more likely, however, that he simply gave them a vast sum of money. Spartacus was not short on money and resources, thanks to the relentless plundering of his army. He probably paid the pirates and then relied on a pirate's honor. Of which, it would soon transpire, there was none.

The day came for the pirates to arrive and load up Spartacus' men to take them to greener pastures. There must have been a buzz in the rebel camp that day, a hint of excitement despite their distrust of the pirates. Instead of being trapped between Crassus and the sea, there was hope now. They were going somewhere that Spartacus had told them was better. They were going to take one step closer to freedom, just as soon as the swift little pirate ships would begin to appear on the horizon, making the waves bristle with masts.

But the ships never came. Whatever payment Spartacus had given them, the pirates had taken it and disappeared to wherever the swift seas would take them. The rebels were on their own.

Chapter 11 – Crassus' Wall

Even the dark cell of Capua had not left Spartacus feeling as securely and completely trapped as he was right now.

The Thracian had achieved so much in the nearly three years since his last time standing in the gladiatorial arena. He'd been a mock hero of entertainment then, killing others like him for the enjoyment of the bloodthirsty crowd. But ever since he and his followers had seized kitchen knives and fled from their prison, he had become something far more. He had become a real hero to real people in a real life-and-death situation. The battles of the gladiators had been staged, even though the spilled blood had been all too real. Yet every drop of Roman blood that stained all of Italy from the Alps to Rhegium had been spilled for a reason, for the sake of freedom, at least in Spartacus' mind. Freedom had been the tantalizing hope that had drawn him every step of the way.

And it was freedom now that he had lost. He might be a real hero to the rebels now, a kind of legend, but he feared that he would never be the one thing he really wanted to be: free. An ordinary Thracian living an ordinary life on the high plateau where he had run and played as a boy. He rued the day that he had become a Roman soldier.

The Cilician pirates had been Spartacus' trump card, his last hope, but now, that hope was gone. Because Crassus had caught up.

It's easy to imagine Crassus practically cackling with glee when he saw the predicament that his worthy adversary had gotten himself into. Spartacus might not have been holed up in a town—or upon the flank of an active volcano—but his position on the peninsula of Bruttium left him almost as vulnerable to a siege as if he had chosen to bring his army into a city. That was, if Crassus could do the impossible: build a wall across the entire peninsula, a wall that would have been forty miles long.

Even as Spartacus scrambled to find a way out, Crassus was busy sealing off his only hope of escape. Crassus' men were driven by a force even more powerful than the hope that Spartacus was offering his people: fear. Knowing that they had to fight or die, they strove to build the enormous wall, complete with a fifteen-foot ditch at the foot of it, in a matter of days.

Spartacus believed the only way to escape was to head toward Sicily. He ordered his men to begin building rafts, made by lashing planks to empty barrels; lumber was cut wherever it could be found, and shipbuilding was attempted. But the rafts were washed out to sea by the fast-flowing waters of the strait, and so, the attempts were abandoned. Some sources claim that Crassus took measures to put a stop to the shipbuilding, although his methods are not described.

Winter came thick and cold that year. The temperatures plummeted, and the balmy summers that had been so good to Spartacus and his men were gone now, reducing fertile Bruttium into what felt like a bare and icy wasteland. Snow fell among the rebel camp and turned to slush, trampled by the feet of men and horses. There were very little provisions left for the men, as Bruttium had already been stripped almost bare, and there was even less grazing for the horses. Crassus, smug and safe behind his ramparts, knew that he would barely have to fight the rebels at all.

Starvation would be his weapon, and he would wield it with a far greater skill than Claudius Glaber had at the feet of Vesuvius.

It was as if the presence of the wall somehow dimmed the golden glow of Spartacus' charisma. Faced with hunger and death, the men had lost hope, and they had lost faith in their leader after his decision to trust the pirates. Cracks began to appear in the cohesion with which Spartacus' men had operated in the early days. The men were hungry, desperate, and terrified. Spartacus knew that it was only their tenacity and fire that had brought them this far, and if he lost those two qualities, then the war would be over. He needed to strike now, hard and fast, not only to gain freedom but to regain morale. It was all they had left.

One night, a snowstorm descended upon the two encamped armies, and Crassus felt a rush of relief and excitement as he watched the white flakes cascade thickly down onto the slumbering landscape. His men had ample food and firewood; the rebels, on the other hand, had been trapped for some time now, and they would have stripped the landscape utterly bare of warmth or sustenance. Surely this snowstorm would be enough to break them. Those left alive in the morning would come crawling to him for surrender, and he would go home to Rome, and the consuls would give him a triumph, and he would finally be on equal footing with Pompey.

Crassus, however, had underestimated one thing about the rebels: their toughness. These were not Roman legionaries who had been given a carefully calculated ration, trained in exactly the right way, or grown up in homes with food and freedom. These men used to be slaves. They were used to being punished for exhaustion by being given more work and less food. They were used to being beaten and starved. They were used to being trapped, and as much as it panicked them, it could not crush them. A mere snowstorm was nothing compared with the icy rage they'd often experienced at the hands of their masters, and so when Spartacus gave one more rousing speech, rallying his army one more time, they rose up and followed him.

None of the Roman legionaries were expecting it when the sound of marching feet among howling snow on the other side of the wall turned out to be the rebel army. Despite being half-blinded by the blizzard, the slaves were attacking. Somehow traversing the massive ditch, they scaled the wall with the same quick agility as they had used rappelling down the cliffs of Mount Vesuvius. Spartacus was leading them personally, and his sword flashed in his hand, snowflakes scattering on his cloaked shoulder, as he struck down one Roman soldier after another. Reinforcements were slow to gather, and by the time the legions could pull themselves together, Spartacus' army was gone: it had melted away into the snowstorm, disappearing but for their tracks. And with the snow coming down fast, even those were almost impossible to follow.

Once again, the rebels had slipped through Crassus' clutches, and Spartacus had access once more to southern Italy. Now perhaps, at last, he could drive north, as hard and as fast as possible, to reach the Alps by the time spring broke and finally break free into the land that he loved and missed. At this point, most classical historians agree that Spartacus' heart was set on nothing but going home. There were many obstacles between the great Thracian and Thrace itself, but at least now he was traveling in the right direction.

But once again, the greatest of those obstacles would prove to be disunity in Spartacus' own ranks. The Germans and Gauls among them—many of them the same men who had followed Crixus in that first fateful split—didn't want to return to Thrace. They still believed that Rome could be conquered, even despite the setbacks they had lately suffered. This time, Spartacus refused to comply with them. He was going north, and if the Germans and Gauls wanted to get themselves killed, then that was their choice. With most of the Thracians following him, Spartacus kept pushing north, putting distance between himself and the Roman legions.

It was just as well. Crassus had been surprised by the attack in the snowstorm, and he was enraged by the fact that Spartacus had escaped. Terrified of decimation, his troops raced after Spartacus, determined to catch him. Almost demented by jealousy and rage, Crassus was driving them on harder than ever, knowing that it wouldn't be long before Pompey returned.

But they didn't catch up with Spartacus—at least, not at first. Instead, they caught up with the group of Germans and Gauls that Spartacus had left behind. Whether or not they had been expecting tens of thousands of Roman legionaries to come marching down upon them, the group of rebels was not ready to fight them. Even Spartacus knew better than to engage Crassus in a pitched battle; it was why he had attempted his escape in a snowstorm instead of attacking the wall under more favorable conditions. The event that followed was less of a battle than it was a downright disaster. Twelve thousand three hundred rebels perished, cut down mercilessly by the Roman legionaries, and Crassus went on to pursue the rest of Spartacus' army.

Spartacus, meanwhile, had come across the Roman vanguard. It's unspecified how many men were in this vanguard, although the name of its commanding officer is known, a cavalryman named Lucius Quinctius. Quinctius had been attempting to pursue Spartacus ever since he had slipped past him after escaping from the wall, and Spartacus eventually turned back to attack him. This time, with the battle being fought in a series of quick guerrilla movements, Spartacus' army was successful. The vanguard was defeated, and Spartacus and his men were able to keep heading north. Quinctius survived the attack and went on to become a successful politician, but he was never known for his military efforts.

Who knows whether they would have made it, scrambling through Italy as they had done before, all the way back to the Alps? Who knows whether Spartacus might have been able to go home instead of standing by the mountains, like Moses, gazing into the untouchable Promised Land? Perhaps they might have, if they'd been able to keep going. But once again, for reasons unknown, the rebel army came crashing to a halt after the defeat of the Roman vanguard.

Even classical historians could only guess at what caused Spartacus to stop where he did, once again on the very precipice of freedom. Much of it may have had to do with the fact that Spartacus' ragtag rebel army was simply exhausted, incapable of going a step farther after the arduous winter they had suffered. Some historians speculate that the victory over the Roman vanguard had once again gone to the rebels' heads. They may have hoped that all their struggles were merely temporary setbacks and that they could still defeat Crassus if Spartacus would only lead them. Yet most historians agree, and it would appear, that Spartacus himself wanted nothing more than to head back toward the Alps.

Whatever happened, the rebel army came to a halt on the banks of the Silarius River. It is very plausible that the rebels wanted to bring the fight to Crassus, and if that was the case, Spartacus was faced with a terrible choice. Should he do once more what he had done with Crixus, and with the other band of Germans and Gauls, and leave them to the fate they'd chosen? Spartacus could have easily chosen to take a few sympathizers and flee north; the remaining men might have slowed Crassus down long enough for Spartacus, at least, to make his escape. But Crixus had already been killed, and so had the others that Spartacus had left behind. He wouldn't have any more of the rebels' blood on his conscience. So, fatally, Spartacus decided to stay.

As he'd done after the death of Crixus, however, Spartacus committed a dark and ironic act after hearing about the deaths of the 12,300 men. Perhaps in a last bid to dissuade his men from fighting Crassus in open battle, or perhaps simply to fuel their fighting spirit, he ordered that one of the Roman prisoners be brought to him. A cross was made by nailing together two long planks of wood. Then the prisoner, bound and held down, was dragged onto the cross. A single nail was driven through his ankles and into the wood; two more were hammered painfully through the long tendons of his wrists. Blood soaked the wood and ran down his skin, and as he screamed in agony, the rebels hauled the cross upright. And the Roman hung crucified against the gray winter sky, dying slowly and in terrible agony as Spartacus' whole army watched.

Spartacus turned to his troops and told them that if they stayed, if they fought, and if they lost, then this was what would happen to them. They would be crucified, and they would die the ugliest, most painful death imaginable. Crassus would make sure of that.

But the men stayed. And Spartacus was faced one last time with the deadliest choice of all: fight or die.

Chapter 12 – The Last Stand

Illustration IV: The death of Spartacus as imagined by Nicola Sanesi

On the banks of the Silarius, under the shadow of the crucified Roman, Spartacus drew his sword. The gray sky gave it a dull gleam; the blade was scratched and notched, scarred much like the man who wielded it. He stood beside his proud cavalry horse—perhaps the same one they had captured from Varinius, which would have felt like a lifetime ago—and with one swift strike, he killed it. The beautiful animal fell to the ground with a thud that every man in Spartacus' army felt in their bones. He turned to them with hollow eyes, the dark blood of the horse spreading through the iced ground at his feet.

"If we win this battle," he said calmly, "I will have my choice of horses. But if we lose, I will have no more need of a horse."

Spartacus knew that day that he was walking into a battle to the very death. It was the only way he knew how to live: let alone fight or die, he knew he had to win or die. And as Crassus' eight legions waited for the rebels with a quiet patience that nonetheless hummed with power, Spartacus knew that there was no way he could win. The fools who loved him, who followed him, had made one mistake too many. They should have crossed the Alps a year ago.

But they hadn't. They were here now, facing the Roman legions in a pitched battle, and there was nothing that Spartacus could do about it. Ever since breaking through the ramparts, Spartacus knew he had been steadily losing control over his men. The sight of Crassus' army showing up and setting itself in array against the rebels had already caused several small groups of rebels to break off from the main army and attack Crassus without Spartacus' command, always ending in tragedy.

Even Spartacus had, for the first time, considered that there might be an option other than to fight or die. He sent messengers to Crassus, hoping to make peace with his enemy; the Roman army, for all its might, had also suffered much that winter, and Spartacus hoped that Crassus would opt for a quick peace. But the Roman's goal was not to make peace. It was to gain glory, and even though making a truce with Spartacus could have saved thousands of lives, Crassus wasn't interested in conserving human life—as he had clearly demonstrated in his decimation of the troops. He was interested in winning, in being as glorious and as praised and admired as Pompey. And the only way that was going to happen was if he utterly defeated and annihilated the wily Thracian who faced him.

Crassus was also aware that Pompey had already returned to Rome; in fact, the Senate had sent him and his war-hardened legions straight toward Bruttium. As Crassus prepared for battle with Spartacus, Pompey was already on his way. If the richest man in Rome was going to get his glorious military victory, he had to do it quickly, before Pompey reached them and claimed the glory for ending the war.

So, Spartacus was truly out of options. There would be no more surprise attacks on Crassus, no more guerilla warfare. There was only one thing left to do, and it was the last thing that Spartacus wanted: a pitched battle. He hoped that by using two grisly actions—the crucifixion of the Roman and the killing of his horse—he would inspire the rebels as well as he could. It felt like a last resort.

And then he charged into battle.

On foot, sword in his hand, Spartacus rushed forth, and the tidal wave of the rebels (what was left of them, anyway) came crashing after him. Spartacus headed for one particular spot in the line, the place where Crassus himself was standing, surrounded by centurions. In those moments, all that Spartacus could think of was his hatred. Hatred for this man who'd turned the tide of a war that had looked so promising. Hatred for this pompous Roman, a man who already had everything that Spartacus had ever dreamed of, a home, a family, a wife, the freedom to do and become whatever he wanted, the freedom to be wherever he wanted. But it hadn't been enough for Crassus. The basic rights that Spartacus had been fighting for weren't enough for him. Not even his overwhelming wealth was enough for him, wealth that gave him the freedom to do as he pleased. No, Crassus needed glory, too, and because of his need for praise and admiration, because of his arrogance, Spartacus wasn't ever going to go home. He knew it deep down. But maybe, if he fought hard enough, he'd give Crassus what he deserved—a death at the edge of a sword.

All around Spartacus, the sounds of battle dissolved into a fog of madness and fear. There were clashes and screams, feet and hooves thundering and churning on the icy earth. Armor and weapons flashed at him as he continued his charge, and he shoved them all aside, even when the hot blood of his own comrades sprayed against his face. He made straight for Crassus, for the centurions surrounding him, fighting with that desperation that had kept him alive in the gladiatorial arena.

Maybe Spartacus believed that if he killed Crassus, the Roman troops would realize they had no one left to fear. Maybe they'd give up, and he could go free after all. Either way, it was with desperation and rage that he finally reached the centurions guarding Crassus and crossed blades with them. The legions began to close in around Spartacus and the men nearest him, but he fought on, slashing and stabbing, turning and striking, a whirlwind of rage and death, and the centurions' blood splashed on his armor. He killed two of them, and then there was nothing standing between him and Crassus. The courageous gladiator and the jealous praetor faced each other for an instant, and Spartacus was ready to strike.

But Spartacus and Crassus, by all accounts, would never actually exchange blows. Instead, one of the other Romans struck first. He slashed Spartacus in the leg, opening an ugly wound that poured blood onto the icy ground. The rebel leader fell to his knees, unable to rise, but he still refused to surrender. Striking upward at the wave of enemies that kept on coming at him, he killed several more Roman soldiers before they were everywhere, butchering his men and surrounding him. And even then, he fought to his last movement, to his last strike.

To the last beat of his heart.

The Battle of the Silarius River, fought on an unknown date in early 71 BCE, was less of a battle than it was simply a massacre. Only one thousand Romans perished, while Spartacus' force was utterly destroyed. Some of the rebels escaped into the mountains, but the vast majority of them were killed in numbers so great that their corpses lay strewn everywhere on the battlefield. One of those corpses belonged to Spartacus. The road from Capua, for all his courage and brilliance, had led him to a mass grave in Italy. He would never see Thrace again. Not even his bones would rest under Thracian stars, as Spartacus' body was never even identified. Along with the thousands of his fellow rebels—the men he'd refused to leave behind, the men he'd fought and died for—he was cast into a mass grave and forgotten. The grave still lies unmarked somewhere at the mouth of the modern-day Sele River. He was only around forty years old when he died.

The bones of one of the world's greatest heroes rotted away among the corpses of his followers, beneath the spot where he had both fought and died.

Chapter 13 – Aftermath

The Third Servile War was over, and Spartacus was dead. But even for Marcus Licinius Crassus, this could hardly be counted as a victory.

Oh, the Romans won, that much was indisputable. The rebels were not so much defeated as they were simply slaughtered. It's also difficult to imagine how it would have been done without Crassus' brutal yet effective command. The disunity in Spartacus' ranks certainly contributed to the problem, but Crassus, savage as he was, was the only commander who took Spartacus seriously enough that he could finally be forced into pitched battle and defeated.

But as far as Crassus was concerned, the victory came just a little too late. The battle was likely still in full swing when suddenly the horizon was covered in red and silver. Legionaries came marching in by the thousands, their strong rectangular shields held up, their ranks bristling with spears like the quills on a gigantic porcupine. It was Pompey. He'd arrived from Rome just in time, according to him, to save the day. Crassus' legions had left only small groups of scattered rebels, and Pompey busily set to work cleaning them up. The exhausted and battered ranks of Crassus' army had done the bulk of the work, and Crassus knew he had been the commander who ended the Third Servile War. But once again, Pompey arrived to steal the glory right out from under his nose.

Pompey captured thousands of rebels. They were without their leader now, scattered in ragged bunches everywhere, no longer even attempting to fight the Romans. For three glorious years, these men had been rebels. But the loss of Spartacus had reduced them to panicked sheep without a shepherd; they weren't rebels or revolutionaries anymore. They were just escaped slaves, lost and terrified, and they were cut down in the thousands by Pompey's troops. Most of them were fleeing north, back toward Capua along the Appian Way, which is perhaps ironic considering that it was at Capua that the war truly started. Seventy-eight men had fled from there with kitchen knives in 73 BCE. Now, six thousand men were fleeing back in that direction, pursued by hostile Romans.

And they were captured. And once they were captured, these slaves were not returned to their owners. Pompey and Crassus both knew that an example would have to be made out of them. The stories about the Spartacus rebellion had sparked unrest among the still-captive slaves all across the Roman Republic, and there were so many of them that if all of those slaves decided to rise up—if another Spartacus appeared to lead them—then they could possibly outnumber their masters and overwhelm them. This was the third servile war in less than a hundred years, and Pompey decided that this time, it would be the last. He would make an example out of these rebels, an example so brutal that it would put any thoughts of rebellion to death.

So, he crucified them. Just as Spartacus thought would happen.

And it was not just one or two of the prisoners. No, Pompey crucified every single man and woman that he captured, lining the length of the Appian Way with wooden crosses and struggling, gasping, dying rebels. All the way from Rome to Brindisi, the great road was flanked by gory death. The Romans left them there to die—sometimes it took days—as they went on to pursue more of the rebels. When they caught them, the Romans would bring them back to the Appian Way, nail them to the wooden crosses, and hoist them into the air. Hanging from the nail holes in their hands, forced to brace themselves against the nail in their ankles to be able to lift their chests and breathe, these men suffered horrifically for hours upon hours until they finally died from asphyxiation or, sometimes, sheer exhaustion. All who passed along the Appian Way saw their naked corpses hanging there, some of them still breathing, some screaming, but their eyes all lifeless with suffering. They had hoped for freedom, but what they gained was a slow and agonizing death.

Six thousand rebels were crucified along that road during the beginning of 71 BCE. And their six thousand bodies were left to hang on the crosses until the bodies rotted away. The seasons came and went, and the skeletons were bleached white, as the wind rattled them and blew through the empty ribcages, singing mournfully to the slaves of the Roman Republic that freedom was nothing but a dream. A foolish, deadly dream.

They lined the road from Capua to Rome like a ghostly honor guard for their dead general. And Pompey's plan worked: there would never be a servile war in Rome again.

As for the gladiatorial games, their time was just beginning. They would only reach the height of their popularity almost five hundred years later, where thousands of them would fight each other at a time for the enjoyment of the masses. They were finally stopped by Emperor Honorius in 404 CE.

* * *

Crassus never got the triumph that he dreamed of. Just as he had expected, Pompey was given all of the credit for ending the Third Servile War. Yet another glorious triumph was thrown across the streets of Rome for him, and the crowds sang his praises as he rode in a chariot like modern-day royalty. Crassus was given only a motley little ovation—a simple parade on foot through a small section of Rome. And while it was still a significant honor, it planted a seed of blazing hatred in Crassus' heart. He had been the one who did all the work of putting down the Spartacus rebellion, and he knew it. Pompey's role in the war had simply been that of chasing down a few remaining rebel elements. Crassus had whipped all of those legions into shape, led them against Spartacus, built a forty-mile wall to lay siege to an entire peninsula, and even decimated his own army in order to defeat the gladiator general. Yet, even so, he was given almost no military recognition. The people of Rome still viewed Spartacus' rebellion as something of an embarrassment, especially now that the actual threat had faded from their memories. Defeating Sertorius in Spain held much greater prestige, and Pompey was hailed as a hero, while Crassus was barely recognized at all. Crassus tried to make up for this with a series of lavish celebratory banquets, but he never gained the title of "Great" that Pompey carried.

The frustration and ignominy resulting from this lack of recognition would pursue Crassus for the rest of his life, never allowing him to rest from the black shadow of jealousy that nipped at his heels. All through his life, he would continue to compete with Pompey for popularity and prestige, and he would never quite win.

In 70 BCE, both Crassus and Pompey were elected as consuls. They were forced to work together, which they did begrudgingly, making numerous political reforms and weeding corruption out of the Senate. Crassus appears to have been a fairly able consul, but he just couldn't compare with Pompey in the following years. Where his illustrious rival set off on military conquests, Crassus was elected as a censor, a task at which he failed miserably. He was sent to annex Egypt and, when he proved incapable of doing so, he was removed from his position.

Pompey, meanwhile, was tasked with finally weeding out the Cilician pirates once and for all. These pirates had been terrorizing Rome for decades, and putting a stop to their activities took

Pompey only three months. In fact, Pompey was able to relocate the pirates to more inland towns, where most of them were integrated into productive society and lived peaceful lives as farmers. He followed that up by heading toward Armenia, where he conquered Tigranes the Great and helped to end the last of the Mithridatic Wars. He became the darling of Rome, its leading military hero. Crassus' defeat of Spartacus was all but forgotten.

Even his political career appeared to be almost over thanks to his bumbling failure as a censor. He had, however, formed an alliance in the late 60s BCE with a young man who would prove to be more legendary than Pompey, Crassus, and Spartacus put together: Julius Caesar. None the worse off for his encounter with the Cilician pirates, Caesar was angling to become a consul, and Crassus and Pompey both worked together to back him. When he was elected in 59 BCE, his alliances with Crassus and Pompey resulted in the First Triumvirate. The Roman Republic was dying, and Crassus was now one of the leading figures in its swansong.

Crassus' wealth was, by this point, almost impossibly huge. He was also one of the three most powerful men in Rome. But he still hadn't proven himself on the battlefield, and his wealth and power were nothing to him without fame and popularity. As a part of the Triumvirate, he was sent to Syria as its governor, and it was here that he was finally given an opportunity to prove himself once more.

Rome had been at war with Parthia—modern-day Iran—for decades. And Crassus jumped at the chance to go to battle with the Parthian king, Orodes II. 54 BCE proved to be a good year for Crassus' campaign; he pushed Orodes out of Armenia and seemed to be finally winning the war. If he could end the war with Parthia, he would be given even greater glory than Pompey could ever achieve.

But he didn't. Crassus grew overambitious, blinded by his quest for greatness. He launched a daring attack into the heart of Parthia itself without enough men, even though his son had already been killed in battle and the Armenian king, a former Roman ally, had deserted them. Now well into middle age, Crassus was no longer the commander that he had been when he was fighting the Third Servile War almost twenty years ago. He led his legions right into the range of Orodes II's swift horseback archers, who were more than a match for the lumbering Romans. Quickly surrounding the Romans, Orodes' archers subjected them to a rain of arrows so thick that the legionaries could barely see. Those left alive were forced to surrender, not only their weapons but also their banner.

Losing their banner was a disgrace even greater than throwing down one's weapons in flight. For Crassus, it was an unbearable humiliation. Perhaps he would have found some sense of relief in the fact that he wouldn't be able to go back to Rome and face the degradation of those whose admiration he sought so fiercely. Crassus would never set foot in his city or spend a single aureus of his wealth ever again because Orodes killed him in 53 BCE. Legend has it that he had liquid gold poured down his throat so that he suffocated and burned in the metal for which he'd made so many corrupt choices. It's more likely that he was executed or just plain killed in battle, though.

Either way, Crassus would never become the hero he wanted to be. And shortly afterward, it was Pompey himself who would march across Armenia and conquer the Parthians, cleaning up Crassus' mess one last time.

Chapter 14 – Legacy

Illustration V: The Bolshoi Ballet depicts Spartacus in chains

"In overthrowing me, you have cut down only the trunk of the Tree of Liberty." The words were delivered through gritted teeth, his brown eyes blazing with defiance. "It will spring up again by the roots for they are numerous and deep."

These words, uttered by Toussaint L'Ouverture (also spelled as Louverture) of Saint Domingue, were as prophetic as they were defiant. The revolutionary and former slave had risen up in 1791, inspired by the French Revolution, to overthrow the Frenchmen who had dominion over him and his brothers. The French

Revolution had come and gone, but the revolution in Saint Domingue continued on, freeing half a million slaves as they overthrew the French, the British, and the Spanish. And this man, this defiant black man who dared to spit in the eye of Napoleon himself, had led it. In fact, where he stood now before Napoleon, Toussaint L'Ouverture was the governor-general of both Saint Domingue—later to be named Haiti—and Hispaniola, the modern-day Dominican Republic.

L'Ouverture had led the only successful slave revolt in modern history. It was thanks to the fact that slaves outnumbered free people ten to one on the island, and also to L'Ouverture's excellent military command, that all three of the great empires that had come to fight him had been defeated. The British had died of yellow fever, the French had succumbed in battle, and the Spanish had been unable to keep L'Ouverture out of Hispaniola. The man was unstoppable, but so was Napoleon. And it was Napoleon who stopped him. L'Ouverture would die of pneumonia in a French prison in 1803. His jailer refused to allow physicians near him, saying that because he was black, and therefore wholly different, the European doctors wouldn't know how to treat him.

The revolution, however, did not die with L'Ouverture. It lived on beyond him, just as he had prophesied. On New Year's Day, 1804, Haiti became an independent country. France begrudgingly recognized its independence. This came sixty years before the American Civil War would put an end to slavery in the United States of America, and it came one hundred years before Cuba would throw off its Spanish shackles and declare equality and freedom. Haiti was one of the first, and L'Ouverture led it into the dawn of freedom.

For that reason, they called him the "Black Spartacus."

* * *

Toussaint L'Ouverture was not the only man to invoke the name of Spartacus in his quest for freedom. To this day, the gladiator general has left a legacy of courage and sacrifice in the name of freedom that has lived on in historical events and popular culture alike.

Karl Marx was one of Spartacus' great fans; his later revolutionary admirer, Che Guevara, would also see Spartacus as a hero. Guevara was an important part of the Cuban Revolution, an event that would change the course of history not only in Cuba but also in the rest of the world, as it placed communist leader Fidel Castro in charge of the island, which is located just ninety miles from Florida. Spartacus had been dead for a little over two thousand years, but he was still hailed as a hero by those who saw themselves as fighting for freedom against an arrogant aristocracy; in the case of the Cuban Revolution, corrupt President Fulgencio Batista was an ideal—and eerie—echo of rich and jealous Crassus.

Guevara was not the only Marxist to proclaim himself to be a follower of the long-dead Spartacus. In post-WWI Germany, the so-called Spartacist Revolt caused chaos in Berlin in January 1919. After the abdication of Kaiser Wilhelm II after World War I ended in defeat for Germany, a socialist republic was founded, and Marxist leaders Karl Liebknecht and Rosa Luxemburg decided to try and tip the scales toward full-blown communism. Liebknecht and Luxemburg had suffered during the First World War, and both ended up in prison shortly thereafter, having been arrested for treason in 1916. Upon their release two years later, they formed what they called the Spartacist League. Like Guevara and Castro, they saw communism as a solution for oppression by an aristocratic minority, and they named themselves after the famed gladiator general with visions of freedom.

Sadly, for Liebknecht and Luxemburg, their bid for what they perceived as freedom would be just as unsuccessful as that of Spartacus. Although their revolt succeeded in capturing numerous important buildings in Berlin, their supporters were ultimately no match for the German military. Hundreds of Spartacists were shot and killed; many of these were in an execution-style after the revolutionaries had already laid down their weapons. Liebknecht was shot. Luxemburg had her skull bashed in and was cast into the river by a bunch of derisive soldiers. Germany freed itself from the clutches of communism and attempted to establish a democracy, but of course, the worst was yet to come for this country. Hitler and the Nazis were on their way.

Not all of the events inspired by Spartacus were grim ones, however. Although the German Spartacists were not the last to call themselves by that name—there were groups in the United States and the United Kingdom with similar ethos who also called themselves Spartacists in the 1970s—Spartacus' legacy lives on in popular culture as well. The courageous story of a gladiator who tried to overthrow an entire government still captures the imagination of the world.

Perhaps the earliest writer to create a work of fiction based on Spartacus' extraordinary life was Raffaello Giovagnoli with his 1874 novel, *Spartacus*. Many more would follow: Arthur Koestler's *The Gladiators*, Lewis Grassic Gibbon's *Spartacus*, and Halina Rudnicka's *The Students of Spartacus*.

In 1960, Stanley Kubrick's film *Spartacus* embellished the story, but it nonetheless brought this piece of history to life on the big screen for the first time. It was the recipient of an Academy Award and also created the famous "I'm Spartacus!" quote. As rousing as the scene may have been, there is sadly no historical evidence to support the story of hundreds of Spartacus' followers rising up to prevent their leader's capture.

Spartacus' tale would also inspire a ballet, which was composed in 1956 by Aram Khachaturian, an Armenian. The ballet was based on Giovagnoli's novel, but like the novel, its ties to real events were strong ones. Khachaturian's words about the ballet perhaps best summarize how Spartacus' story has influenced both history and culture throughout the two thousand years following his failed rebellion. "I thought of *Spartacus* as a monumental fresco describing the mighty avalanche of the antique rebellion of slaves on behalf of human rights...When I composed the score of the ballet and tried to capture the atmosphere of ancient Rome in order to bring to life the images of the remote past, I never ceased to feel the spiritual affinity of Spartacus to our own time."

Spiritual or not, for centuries, the struggle of Spartacus has been one that the modern world has had an affinity with, and for good reason. Spartacus' rebellion might not have been about abolition, but it was still about freedom. It was still about struggling out of the clutches of a powerful enemy. Spartacus might not have been dreaming about a Roman Republic where no one would ever be enslaved again. But he was dreaming about walking free under the Thracian stars. He was dreaming of going home, and at the very heart of all struggles for human rights, home and freedom are still their themes.

Conclusion

Slavery would only end in the Roman Empire when it gradually faded out of existence during the latter years of the Empire, but even then, it eventually turned into serfdom, which was barely any better. All across the world, for thousands of years to follow, slaves would continue to fight for their freedom. Many simply fought to escape slavery, like Spartacus and his men did. But in later years, freedom fighters would rise up who sought to abolish slavery altogether.

Slavery did not die with the Roman Empire. Throughout the Middle Ages, slaves were still common throughout most of the world. In Europe, slavery was largely replaced with the feudal system, in which serfs worked for free and had their lives generally controlled by their lords—a kind of bondage hardly better than slavery itself.

The discovery of the Americas and the colonization of Africa brought about slavery on a scale that ancient Rome could never even have dreamed of. When Portuguese traders began the transatlantic slave trade in 1444, they ushered in an era of the most horrific exploitation of man by his own fellow man that the world has ever seen. The transatlantic slave trade would rip around 12.5 million African people from the country where they'd grown up, forcibly relocate them to the New World, and put them to work in countries that were filled with peril. From abusive masters to diseases for which they had no immunity, those slaves who lived long enough to reach the New World lived appalling and dangerous lives. The tide only began to turn in 1781, which was when slavery was first abolished in the Holy Roman Empire. The French Revolution (and the subsequent Haitian Revolution) in the late 18th and early 19th centuries were fuel to the flame of abolition.

It was only in 1848, however, that one of the prominent colonial powers would abolish slavery in all of its New World colonies. Ironically, considering it was a French emperor who killed L'Ouverture, this power was France during its Second Republic. Spain, Great Britain, and the United States reluctantly followed. Finally, in 1888, slavery in the New World mostly ended when the Golden Law was passed, abolishing slavery in South America.

In the modern day, slavery is finally illegal in every recognized country across the globe. That's not to say it doesn't exist anymore, however. Twenty-one million people—almost twice the number that crossed the Atlantic Ocean on slave ships—are still living in some form of slavery. Child trafficking, forced labor, bonded labor, and forced marriage are only some of the ways in which millions of people all over the world are still being exploited as slaves. Fifty-five percent of these are women, and about twenty-five percent are children.

The atrocity lives on. But it no longer dares to walk in the sunlight. Spartacus was only the first in a long line of heroes who continue to campaign bravely against this dark monster, this disgusting atrocity against humanity. Toussaint L'Ouverture, Frederick Douglass, Abraham Lincoln, Olaudah Equiano, William Wilberforce—their names ring down through the distance of the centuries as those who dared to stand against that monster. And Spartacus was their leader, the first of them all.

This courageous Roman gladiator may not have planned to abolish slavery. The very concept of abolition would have been an utterly foreign one to him; the Roman economy and culture were so deeply entrenched in the practice of slavery that the absence of slavery was almost inconceivable.

Spartacus didn't make lengthy speeches about human rights. In fact, human rights weren't even something that people thought about in the Roman Republic. But he did know the struggle for freedom that so many great men and women would share in during later centuries. He knew, perhaps not as intellectually as Abraham Lincoln or Harriet Tubman, that the exploitation of one human being by another was wrong, painful, and cruel. He knew that he didn't want to spend the rest of his life shackled in a Roman cell. He knew that the sound of the wind across the Thracian plateau called him even when that plateau was so far away. And he knew that the tens of thousands—the 120,000, at one point—who followed him also deserved to walk as free men.

He gave his life fighting for a free world. And almost 2,100 years later, courageous individuals still follow in his footsteps, believing in hope. Believing in freedom.

Here's another book by Captivating History that you might like

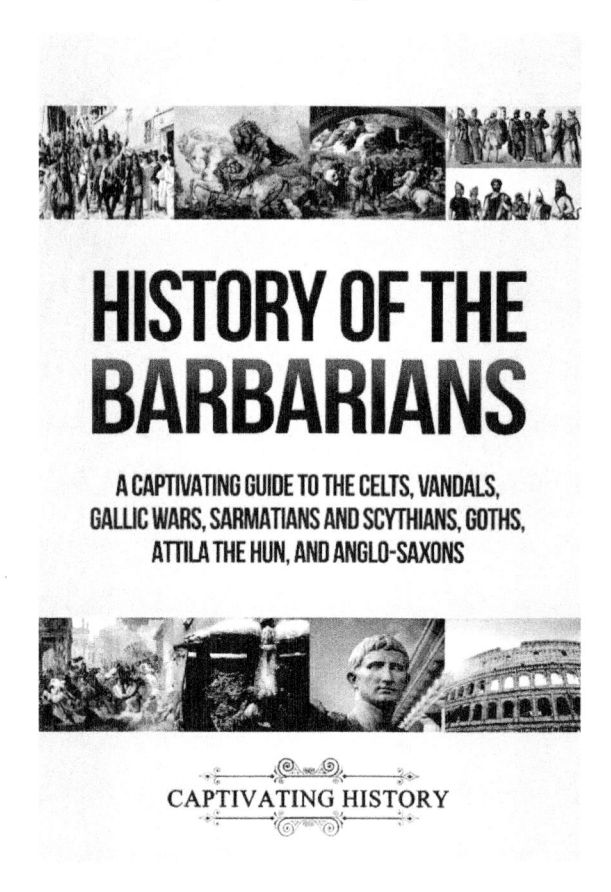

HISTORY OF THE BARBARIANS

A CAPTIVATING GUIDE TO THE CELTS, VANDALS, GALLIC WARS, SARMATIANS AND SCYTHIANS, GOTHS, ATTILA THE HUN, AND ANGLO-SAXONS

CAPTIVATING HISTORY

Free Bonus from Captivating History (Available for a Limited time)

Hi History Lovers!

Now you have a chance to join our exclusive history list so you can get your first history ebook for free as well as discounts and a potential to get more history books for free! Simply visit the link below to join.

Captivatinghistory.com/ebook

Also, make sure to follow us on Facebook, Twitter and Youtube by searching for Captivating History.

Sources

Anti-slavery charities to support today:

Anti-Slavery International: https://antislavery.org/

Polaris Project: www.polarisproject.org

Prajwala: www.prajwalaindia.com

Children's Organization of Southeast Asia: www.cosaasia.org

Urban Light: www.urban-light.org

GoodWeave: www.goodweave.org

The Empower Foundation: www.empowerfoundation.org

To learn more about modern-day slavery and how you can help, visit http://www.thedailymuse.com/education/human-trafficking-the-myths-and-the-realities/

Quantum Future Group 2016, Event 74: Second Servile War; Gaius Marius, Quantum Future Group: The Chronicle of the Fall of the Roman Empire, viewed 23 December 2019, <https://cof.quantumfuturegroup.org/events/74>

Cartwright, M. 2013, Slavery in the Roman World, Ancient History Encyclopedia, viewed 23 December 2019, <http://libraryguides.vu.edu.au/harvard/internet-websites>

"Ancient Roman Slaves: A Life of Bondage" History on the Net © 2000-2019, Salem Media. December 23, 2019 <https://www.historyonthenet.com/ancient-roman-slaves>

Simkin, J. 1997, Slavery in the Roman Empire, Spartacus Educational, viewed 23 December 2019, <https://spartacus-educational.com/ROMslaves.htm>

Violatti, C. 2016, 10 Interesting Facts About Slavery in the Roman Empire, Listverse, viewed 23 December 2019, <https://listverse.com/2016/06/05/10-interesting-facts-about-slavery-in-ancient-rome/>

Editors of Encyclopedia Britannica, 2008, Lucius Cornelius Cinna, Encyclopedia Britannica, viewed 27 December 2019, <https://www.britannica.com/biography/Lucius-Cornelius-Cinna>

Wilmott, T. 2013, Gladiators in Ancient Rome: How did they live and die?, BBC History Magazine, viewed 30 December 2019, <https://www.historyextra.com/period/roman/gladiators-in-ancient-rome-how-did-they-live-and-die/>

Cartwright, M. 2019, Roman Gladiator, Ancient History Encyclopedia, viewed 30 December 2019, <https://www.ancient.eu/gladiator/>

Gill, N.S. "Roman Gladiators." ThoughtCo. https://www.thoughtco.com/roman-gladiators-overview-120901 (accessed December 30, 2019).

Andrews, E. 2018, 10 Things You May Not Know About Roman Gladiators, History, viewed 30 December 2019, <https://www.history.com/news/10-things-you-may-not-know-about-roman-gladiators>

Rickard, J (14 September 2017), SULLA'S SECOND CIVIL WAR, 83-82 BC, http://www.historyofwar.org/articles/wars_sullas_second_civil_war.html

Rickard, J (30 March 2018), L. CORNELIUS CINNA (D.84 BC), HTTP://WWW.HISTORYOFWAR.ORG/ARTICLES/PEOPLE_CINNA.HTML

EDITORS OF ENCYCLOPEDIA BRITANNICA 2019, PRAETOR, ENCYCLOPEDIA BRITANNICA, VIEWED 30 DECEMBER 2019, <HTTPS://WWW.BRITANNICA.COM/TOPIC/PRAETOR>

HUGHES, T. 2017, SERTORIUS: HOW ONE MAN TOOK ON AN EMPIRE, BATTLES OF THE ANCIENTS, VIEWED 30 DECEMBER 2019, <HTTP://TURNINGPOINTSOFTHEANCIENTWORLD.COM/INDEX.PHP/2017/07/24/SERTORIUS-HISPANIA-SUCRO-RIVER/>

MCLAUGHLIN, W. 2016, BATTLE OF MOUNT VESUVIUS, SPARTACUS AND HIS MEN RAPPELLING DOWN A MOUNTAIN, WAR HISTORY ONLINE, VIEWED 30 DECEMBER 2019, <HTTPS://WWW.WARHISTORYONLINE.COM/ANCIENT-HISTORY/BATTLE-MOUNT-VESUVIUS-SPARTACUS-MEN-RAPPELLING-MOUNTAIN.HTML>

Lendering, J. 2019, Decimation, Livius, viewed 31 December 2019, <https://www.livius.org/articles/concept/decimation/>

Military History Now 2014, Removal of a Tenth: A Brief and Bloody History of Decimation, Military History Now.com, viewed 31 December 2019, <https://militaryhistorynow.com/2014/02/26/no-safety-in-numbers-a-brief-history-of-decimation/>

Strauss, B., The Spartacus War, Simon and Schuster 2009

Dimuro, G. 2019, Crixus: Spartacus' Right-Hand Man Who May Have Been the Gladiator Army's Downfall, All That's Interesting, viewed 31 December 2019, <https://allthatsinteresting.com/crixus>

Know the Romans, Roman Weapons & Armor, viewed 2 January 2020, <https://www.knowtheromans.co.uk/Categories/RomanArmy/RomanWeaponsandArmour/>

Ward, C. O., The Ancient Lowly, Рипол Классик 1970

Lendering, J. 2019, Thracians, Livius, viewed 2 January 2020, <https://www.livius.org/articles/people/thracians/#Roman%20Conquest>

Mark, J. J. 2019, Pirates of the Mediterranean, Ancient History Encyclopedia, viewed 7 January 2020, <https://www.ancient.eu/article/47/pirates-of-the-mediterranean/>

Lendering, J. 2019, Cilician Pirates, Livius, viewed 7 January 2020, <https://www.livius.org/articles/people/cilician-pirates/>

Wasson, D. L. 2014, Spartacus, Ancient History Encyclopedia, viewed during December 2019, <https://www.ancient.eu/spartacus/>

Czech, K. P. 1994, Spartacus: The Grecian Slave Warrior who Threatened Rome, Military History Magazine, viewed during December 2019, <https://www.historynet.com/spartacus-the-grecian-slave-warrior-who-threatened-rome.htm>

Cartwright, M. 2013, Marcus Licinius Crassus, Ancient History Encyclopedia, viewed during December 2019, <https://www.ancient.eu/Marcus_Licinius_Crassus/>

Freidani, A. 2019, Money was not enough for Crassus, the richest man in Rome, National Geographic, viewed during December 2019, <https://www.nationalgeographic.com/history/magazine/2019/05-06/crassus-romes-richest-man/>

Mark, J. J. 2016, The Spartacus Revolt, Ancient History Encyclopedia, viewed during December 2019, <https://www.ancient.eu/article/871/the-spartacus-revolt/>

Lendering, J. 2019, Spartacus, Livius, viewed during December 2019, <https://www.livius.org/articles/person/spartacus/>

Gill, N. S. 2019, Biography of Spartacus, a Slave Who Led a Revolt, ThoughtCo, viewed during December 2019, <https://www.thoughtco.com/who-was-spartacus-112745>

Editors of Encyclopedia Britannica, Third Servile War, Encyclopedia Britannica, viewed 7 January 2020, <https://www.britannica.com/event/Gladiatorial-War>

Sutherland, C. 2007, Haitian Revolution (1791-1804), Black Past, viewed 7 January 2020, <https://www.blackpast.org/global-african-history/haitian-revolution-1791-1804/>

Thomson, I. 2004, The Black Spartacus, The Guardian, viewed 7 January 2020, <https://www.theguardian.com/books/2004/jan/31/featuresreviews.guardianreview35>

Cavendish, R. 2009, The Spartacist Uprising in Berlin, History Today, viewed 7 January 2020, <https://www.historytoday.com/archive/spartacist-uprising-berlin>

Schwarm, B., Spartacus, Encyclopedia Britannica, viewed 7 January 2020, <https://www.britannica.com/topic/Spartacus-ballet-by-Khachaturian>

Kelly, A. 2013, Modern-day Slavery: An Explainer, The Guardian, viewed 7 January 2020, <https://www.theguardian.com/global-development/2013/apr/03/modern-day-slavery-explainer>

Illustration I:
https://commons.wikimedia.org/wiki/File:Marcus_Licinius_Crassus.jpg

Illustration II:
https://commons.wikimedia.org/wiki/File:3rd_servile_72_plutarch.png

Illustration III:
https://commons.wikimedia.org/wiki/File:Marmolada,_Italy.jpg

Illustration IV:
https://commons.wikimedia.org/wiki/File:Spartacus_by_Sanesi.jpg

Illustration V: By Bengt Nyman - Flickr: DSC_9865, CC BY 2.0, https://commons.wikimedia.org/w/index.php?curid=30261808

Bradley, Keith, Professor; Resisting Slavery in Ancient Rome (February 2011) Retrieved from
http://www.bbc.co.uk/history/ancient/romans/slavery_01.shtml

Salem Media; Ancient Roman Slaves: A Life of Bondage (September 2021) Retrieved from https://www.historyonthenet.com/ancient-roman-slaves

Garland, Robert Ph.D.; Roman Slavery: Who Were the Roman Slaves? (December 2020) Retrieved from https://www.thegreatcoursesdaily.com/roman-slavery-who-were-the-roman-slaves/

Cartwright, Mark; Slavery in the Roman World (November 2013) Retrieved from https://www.worldhistory.org/article/629/slavery-in-the-roman-world/

Wikipedia; Slavery in Ancient Rome (August 2021) Retrieved from https://en.wikipedia.org/wiki/Slavery_in_ancient_Rome

Wikipedia; First Servile War (September 2021) Retrieved from https://en.wikipedia.org/wiki/First_Servile_War

Military Wiki; First Servile War; Retrieved from https://military.wikia.org/wiki/First_Servile_War

History Wiki; First Servile War; Retrieved from https://historica.fandom.com/wiki/First_Servile_War

Academic Kids; First Servile War; Retrieved from http://academickids.com/encyclopedia/index.php/First_Servile_War

Gill, N. S.; The Sicilian Revolts of Enslaved Persons and Spartacus (September 2018) Retrieved from https://www.thoughtco.com/slave-revolts-or-servile-wars-in-italy-112744

Heritagedaily; Eunus – The Roman Slave Who Declared Himself King (July 2021) Retrieved from https://www.heritagedaily.com/2021/07/eunus-the-roman-slave-who-declared-himself-king/139690

Encyclopedia Britannica Editors; Eunus – Roman Slave (November 2019) Retrieved from https://www.britannica.com/biography/Eunus

Wikipedia; Sicilian Wars (August 2021) Retrieved from https://en.wikipedia.org/wiki/Sicilian_Wars

Wikipedia; Battle of Himera (July 2021) Retrieved from https://en.wikipedia.org/wiki/Battle_of_Himera_(480_BC)

Wikipedia; Treaty of Lutatius (June 2021) Retrieved from https://en.wikipedia.org/wiki/Treaty_of_Lutatius

Wikipedia; Battle of Selinus (August 2021) Retrieved from https://en.wikipedia.org/wiki/Battle_of_Selinus

Wikipedia; Siege of Akragas (July 2021) Retrieved from https://en.wikipedia.org/wiki/Siege_of_Akragas_(406_BC)

Wikipedia; Cleon (June 2021) Retrieved from https://en.wikipedia.org/wiki/Cleon_(revolted_slave)

Author Unknown; The First Slave Revolt Was Led by Eunus; Retrieved from https://www.the-romans.eu/slavery/Slave-revolt.php

Wiedeman, Thomas; Greek and Roman Slavery (1981) Retrieved from http://www.professorcampbell.org/sources/slavewar.html

Barca, Natale; Rome's Sicilian Slave Wars: The Revolts of Eunus and Salvius, 136-132 and 105-100BC (August 2020) Published by Pen and Sword Military

Livius, Titus; The History of Rome; Retrieved from http://www.perseus.tufts.edu/hopper/text?doc=Perseus%3Atext%3A1999.02.0150%3Abook%3D68

Wikipedia; Cimbri (September 2021) Retrieved from https://en.wikipedia.org/wiki/Cimbri

Tsouras, Peter; The Cimbrian War, 113-101 B.C. (March 2014) Retrieved from https://www.historynet.com/cimbrian-war-113-101-b-c.htm

Hughes, Tristan; How Gaius Marius Saved Rome from the Cimbri (February 2020) Retrieved from https://www.historyhit.com/how-gaius-marius-saved-rome-from-the-cimbri/

Wikipedia; Cimbrian War (August 2021) Retrieved from https://en.wikipedia.org/wiki/Cimbrian_War

Wikipedia; Second Servile War (August 2021) Retrieved from https://en.wikipedia.org/wiki/Second_Servile_War#Athenion

Siculus, Diodorus; Book 36; Retrieved from http://attalus.org/translate/diodorus36.html

Wikipedia; Lucius Licinius Lucullus (September 2021) Retrieved from https://en.wikipedia.org/wiki/Lucius_Licinius_Lucullus_(praetor_104_BC)

Wikipedia; Battle of the Silarius River (August 2021) Retrieved from https://en.wikipedia.org/wiki/Battle_of_the_Silarius_River

Wikipedia; Battle of Picenum (May 2021) Retrieved from https://en.wikipedia.org/wiki/Battle_of_Picenum

Wikipedia; Battle of Mount Vesuvius (February 2021) Retrieved from https://en.wikipedia.org/wiki/Battle_of_Mount_Vesuvius

Wikipedia; Battle of Cantenna (July 2021) Retrieved from https://en.wikipedia.org/wiki/Battle_of_Cantenna

UKEssays; Spartacus and the Slave Rebellion in Rome, History Essay (November 2018) Retrieved from https://www.ukessays.com/essays/history/spartacus-and-the-slave-rebellion-in-rome-history-essay.php

Author Unknown; Rome's Third Servile War: One of the First Great Battles Against Slavery (September 2019) Retrieved from https://worldhistory.us/ancient-history/ancient-rome/romes-third-servile-war-one-of-the-first-great-battles-against-slavery.php

Czech, Kenneth P.; Spartacus, The Grecian Slave Warrior Who Threatened Rome (April 1994) Retrieved from https://www.historynet.com/spartacus-the-grecian-slave-warrior-who-threatened-rome.htm

S., Alen; Third Servile War in Roman Republic 73-71 BCE (Spartacus Rebellion) (April 2016) Retrieved from https://www.shorthistory.org/ancient-civilizations/ancient-rome/third-servile-war-in-roman-republic-73-71bc-spartacus-rebellion/

Mark, Joshua J.; The Spartacus Revolt (March 2016) Retrieved from https://www.worldhistory.org/article/871/the-spartacus-revolt/

Encyclopedia Britannica Editors; Third Servile War; Retrieved from https://www.britannica.com/event/Gladiatorial-War

Wikipedia; Third Servile War (August 2021) Retrieved from https://en.wikipedia.org/wiki/Third_Servile_War

Russell; Gladiators of Ancient Rome (February 2011) Retrieved from https://www.carpediemrome.com/gladiators-in-ancient-rome/

Gill, N. S.; Roman Gladiators: A Dangerous Job for a Chance for a Better Life (October 2019) Retrieved from https://www.thoughtco.com/roman-gladiators-overview-120901

Wikipedia; Gladiator (August 2021) Retrieved from https://en.wikipedia.org/wiki/Gladiator

Daily History Editors; What Was the Impact of Spartacus' Uprising on Rome (January 2019) Retrieved from https://dailyhistory.org/What_was_the_impact_of_Spartacus'_uprising_on_Rome

Wikipedia; Spartacus (October 2021) Retrieved from https://en.wikipedia.org/wiki/Spartacus

Yourdictionary; Spartacus; Retrieved from https://biography.yourdictionary.com/spartacus

Unknown Author; Spartacus; Retrieved from https://www.livius.org/articles/person/spartacus/

Jarus, Owen; Spartacus: History of Gladiator Revolt Leader (September 2013) Retrieved from https://www.livescience.com/39730-spartacus.html

Wikipedia; Crixus (May 2021) Retrieved from https://en.wikipedia.org/wiki/Crixus

Dimuro, Gina; Crixus: Spartacus' Right-Hand Man Who May Have Been the Gladiator Army's Downfall (January 2019) Retrieved from https://allthatsinteresting.com/crixus

Wikipedia; Oenomaus (September 2021) Retrieved from https://en.wikipedia.org/wiki/Oenomaus_(rebel_slave)

Livius.org; Plutarch on Spartacus; Retrieved from https://www.livius.org/sources/content/plutarch/plutarchs-crassus/plutarch-on-spartacus/

White, Horace; Appian, The Civil Wars; Retrieved from http://www.perseus.tufts.edu/hopper/text?doc=Perseus:abo:tlg,0551, 017:1:14

Wikipedia; Publius Varinius (July 2021) Retrieved from https://en.wikipedia.org/wiki/Publius_Varinius

Wikipedia; Lucius Gellius (March 2021) Retrieved from https://en.wikipedia.org/wiki/Lucius_Gellius

Wikipedia; Gnaeus Cornelius Lentulus Clodianus (August 2021) Retrieved from https://en.wikipedia.org/wiki/Gnaeus_Cornelius_Lentulus_Clodianus

Williams, Julie; The Third Servile War Timeline (April 2016) Retrieved from https://prezi.com/fhto4b5qjrvn/the-third-servile-war-timeline/

Wikipedia; Quintus Arrius (November 2020) Retrieved from https://en.wikipedia.org/wiki/Quintus_Arrius_(praetor_73_BC)

Wikipedia; Marcus Licinius Crassus (October 2021) Retrieved from https://en.wikipedia.org/wiki/Marcus_Licinius_Crassus

Wikipedia; Pompey (October 2021) Retrieved from https://en.wikipedia.org/wiki/Pompey

Wikipedia; Appian Way (October 2021) Retrieved from https://en.wikipedia.org/wiki/Appian_Way

Schools Wikipedia; History of Slavery (2007) Retrieved from https://www.cs.mcgill.ca/~rwest/wikispeedia/wpcd/wp/h/History_of_slavery.htm

Wikipedia; Slavery in Antiquity (August 2021) Retrieved from https://en.wikipedia.org/wiki/Slavery_in_antiquity